City Breaks
in
Central and Eastern
European Cities

Vienna, Salzburg, Budapest
Prague, Warsaw & Kraków

REG BUTLER

In Association with

THOMSON HOLIDAYS

SETTLE PRESS

Text © 1994 Reg Butler
3rd Edition 1997

First published by Settle Press
10 Boyne Terrace Mews
London W11 3LR

ISBN (Paperback) 1 872876 61 7

Printed by Villiers Publications
19 Sylvan Avenue
London N3 2LE

Foreword

As one of Britain's leading short breaks specialists, we recognise the need for detailed information and guidance for CityBreak travellers. But much more is required than just a listing of museums and their opening times. For a few days, the CityBreak visitor wants to experience the local continental lifestyle.

We are therefore very pleased to work with Reg Butler and Settle Press on this latest edition in the CityBreak series of pocket guide-books.

Reg Butler is one of the pioneers of postwar tourism to Central and Eastern Europe. As a young courier, he conducted seasons of tours - to Vienna and Salzburg in 1954 and 1955; to Budapest throughout summer 1956; and to Prague in the following year. In 1958 he conducted one of the first British tours to Warsaw and Kraków. Since then he has returned many times to the region, writing travel articles for British and American newspapers and magazines.

For this book Reg Butler has collaborated closely with our resident Thomson staff and agents, who have year-round experience of helping visitors enjoy these cities. We're sure you'll find this book invaluable in planning how to make best personal use of your time.

As well as CityBreaks in these cities of Central and Eastern Europe, other books in the series cover Paris, Amsterdam, Rome, Florence, Venice, Madrid, Barcelona, Seville, New York, Washington and Boston. Of course Thomson operate to many other cities in Europe and the Americas from departure points across the UK.

THOMSON CITYBREAKS

Contents

Chapter One

Introduction

1.1 Journey to the heart of Europe

For centuries Vienna was the heart of Central Europe: capital of the Austro-Hungarian empire, with a wealthy and sophisticated aristocracy that rivalled the life-style of Paris or St. Petersburg. Vienna was a major political player on the European stage, where power reached out East to the Russian empire and south through the Balkans to the retreating borders of the Ottoman Turks.

Much of present-day Vienna dates from the height of that Austrian power, evoking the late 19th century when Johann Strauss was king of the waltz, and when the aristocratic court life revolved around the huge Imperial Palace called the Hofburg. This was the central office for the Habsburg empire, which had 54 million inhabitants, 16 different nationalities, 9 different religions.

Much of that cultural mix survives today, even though Austria of the 1990's represents a mere 12% of the old Habsburg empire. Vienna itself has 1.5 million inhabitants out of Austria's 7.5 million population. A highly prosperous city, Vienna still keeps its reputation for charm, welcoming two million tourists a year. Indeed, Vienna rates fourth in tourist popularity among the capitals of Europe – following on London, Paris and Rome.

Vienna is a city set to music - from the grandest of opera through ballet and musical comedy to the nostalgia-packed violins and zithers of a night out amid the village wine-taverns of the Vienna Woods. It has a wealth of museums, including the Art History Museum which ranks high among the greatest galleries of Europe. Within the inner city, little has changed since the ancient walls were removed in the 19th century, to be replaced by the stylish buildings, monuments and parks of the Ring.

But, although the past is the great tourist attraction, Vienna still plays a lively role as the main gateway of Central Europe. Forty international organisations are active in Vienna, including the headquarters of the oil exporters' OPEC. Now that the postwar borders of Eastern Europe have crumbled, Vienna's central position has regained its former dominance.

Multi-centre breaks

For the City Break visitor, Vienna can easily be combined with either Salzburg, Budapest or Prague, to make a highly attractive two-centre package. The Polish cities of Warsaw and Kraków can likewise be linked; or Warsaw with Prague.

Each of these beautiful cities can be reached within a few hours by air, rail or road.

Which city to choose?

Salzburg combines well with Vienna – good sightseeing potential with magnificent *Sound of Music* mountain and lake scenery to contrast with the urban delights of the capital. Indeed, Salzburg is an ideal base for visiting the Salzkammergut (Austrian Lake District) or southern Bavaria by day, with music and good restaurants for evening pleasure.

Wherever Central-Europe freaks are gathered together, discussion can turn on which is the more romantic city – Prague or Budapest.

As the frontier city between Europe and Asia during the Middle Ages, and an Imperial city in the 19th century, Budapest on the Danube is a splendid capital with architectural excitement, French chic and Austrian indulgence (just see the locals scoffing pastries at the famous café Vörösmarty!).

Often billed as 'Paris of the East', Budapest features an excellent cuisine with good wine and wild Gypsy music.

In Prague, the centre is virtually unchanged in character since the 18th century. That's why they chose Prague for filming of *Amadeus*, the life of Mozart. There is gas lighting in narrow streets which have been beautifully restored. The splendid Town Hall Square rates among the most beautiful in Europe, with an ancient astronomical clock for an attention-grabbing performance every hour.

A walk over Charles Bridge – one of the fifteen Prague bridges which crosses the River Vltava – is like a 20th-century stroll into the Middle Ages, with no traffic permitted to disturb the entertainers and craftsmen who have adopted the bridge as their favourite pitch. Prague Castle, dominating the skyline, was founded in 9th century, and converted to an imperial residence in 14th century by Charles 1V, who aimed to make Prague the leading capital of Europe.

A great city for strolling, Prague is the place where any romantic would feel at home. There are candlelit bistro-type restaurants, ancient wine taverns, and cafés where you can just sit and watch the world go by.

On a historic prewar occasion, Britain's prime minister Neville Chamberlain described Czechoslovakia as "a far-off, distant country of which we know so little." In fact, Czechoslovakia had twice the population of Austria.

Today, after long years of East-West division, more City Break visitors are combining sightseeing with the fascination of learning more about the changing way of life in the former Communist countries.

After years of political and economic turmoil in Poland, tourism is now thriving in the cities of Warsaw and Kraków, where historic old centres have been faithfully restored to their original charm.

When to go?

Of the six cities described in this book, Prague is the closest to London – 637 air miles, compared to Salzburg 643 miles, Vienna 780 miles, Budapest 913 miles, Warsaw 890 miles, Kraków 870 miles.

For all these cities, May and June are very attractive months. July and August are the tourism high season. September is heavily booked with Conference traffic. Mid-winters can be very chilly. Prague – home town of Good King Wenceslas – makes a determined pitch for the Christmas trade. Vienna and Budapest also promote very active winter seasons of cultural events, with wonderful choice for music-lovers.

Language problems? Czech, Hungarian and Polish are tough going. Most visitors just learn a few basic words and then give up. In all the cities, people in tourism and catering business have reasonable command of English. Otherwise, German is the most useful second language. Restaurant menus are most likely to be translated into German or English, but rarely into French.

1.2 *Explore the cuisine*

Viennese cuisine is a blend of specialities from all the countries that once made up the Austro-Hungarian Empire, as well as the native Austrian dishes. The culinary flow has been three-way, so that Prague, Budapest and Vienna can offer an interchangeable choice that could be described as Central European cuisine.

Apfelstrudel, Wiener Schnitzel and Sachertorte make a frequent appearance on Czech and Hungarian menus, while Hungarian goulash or pancakes or Czech dumplings are equally available in Vienna. In Salzburg, the cuisine keeps closer to traditional Austrian and German.

Thirst-quenchers

On the drinks list, Austria's white wines from the Wachau district of the Danube have a fragrant bouquet. Much of the new wine – the *Heuriger* – is consumed in wine-taverns on the edge of the Vienna Woods. Otherwise, Austrian restaurants can offer a full range of wines from France, Germany, Hungary and the rest.

In Poland, the lower-cost wines are most likely to be Bulgarian.

In Hungary, the indigenous wines can keep you occupied throughout a holiday, while Czech restaurants rely much more on imports from Hungary and Bulgaria. Czech beer is famed around the world.

A Gespritzter is theoretically half-wine, half-soda. Sometimes they go very light on the wine, heavy on the water. However, on a hot day, a Gespritzter is a very refreshing drink.

Another popular thirst-quencher is apple juice – Apfelsaft. Fresh orange juice is quite expensive. If you ask for water, they'll normally serve mineral water which goes on the bill. But tap water is quite safe.

If you ask for tea, you'll usually get a glass mug with warm water and a tea-bag. If you insist on milk, it will probably be condensed.

Coffeehouse tradition

In all four countries, the coffeehouse lifestyle still flourishes. People go to cafés not merely to quench thirst, but to socialize with friends, or to read the newspapers and weekly magazines.

Many coffeehouses date back several hundred years and still have a special atmosphere in which to relax and watch the world go by. No-one can outstay their welcome. Just sit back and try coffee and a pastry.

Especially in Vienna there's choice of coffee made thirty different ways. But here's a short list which is valid anywhere in Central Europe.

Types of coffee

Melange – Half coffee half milk: probably the most popular variation among visitors.
Brauner – Coffee with a little milk
Mokka – Very strong, black and heavily sweetened
Türkischer – Turkish coffee (thick, strong and sweet)
Kaffee mit Schlag – Coffee with whipped cream
Doppelschlag – Coffee with extra cream
Portion Kaffee – Pot of coffee and jug of hot milk

Reading the menus

Menus in Hungarian or Czech are bewildering, and it's very difficult to guess anything more than an occasional word like 'salat' or 'papriky'.

See sections 4.9 and 5.9 for help in decoding the bill of fare in those languages.

The more up-market restaurants may offer an English-language menu, but German is far more likely. That's easier than trying to decipher Czech, Polish or Hungarian. So here's a basic guide to the German-language menus of Central Europe:

Main dishes:

Brathuhn	Roast chicken
Beinfleisch	Boiled beef
Ente	Duck

Forelle	Trout
G'selchtes	Smoked ham with Sauerkraut
Hendl	Chicken
Kalbfleisch	Veal
Kalbshaxe	Shin of Veal
Lamm	Lamb
Rindfleisch	Beef
Rostbraten	Minute steak with onions
Schinken	Ham
Schweinefleisch	Pork

Vegetables and Side Dishes:

Erdäpfel	Potatoes
Fisolen/Bohnen	Green beans
Kartoffelsalat	Potato salad
Knofel/Knoblauch	Garlic
mit Kraut	with Sauerkraut
Nudeln	Noodles
Reis	Rice
Schwammerl/Pilze	Mushrooms

Desserts and fruits:

Apfel	Apple
Birne	Pear
Erdbeeren	Strawberries
Käse	Cheese
Kirschen	Cherries
Kuchen	Cake or fruit flan
Obers/Sahne	Cream
Salzburger Nockerl	Egg-white soufflé with vanilla sauce
Torte	Layer cake
Zitrone	Lemon

Some cooking terms:

Garniert	Dressed, garnished
Gebacken	Baked
Gebraten	Roasted
Gegrillt	Grilled
Gekocht	Boiled
Geräuchert	Smoked
in Essig	In vinegar
mit Sahne	Creamed
Pochert	Poached

Drinks:

Bier	Beer
Kaffee	Coffee
Milch	Milk
Saft	Juice
Tee	Tea
Wein	Wine

INTRODUCTION

Some Austrian and Central European specialities:

Apple Soup	Apples, cloves, cinnamon, white wine, lemon juice, sugar and extremely thick cream.
Wienerschnitzel	Veal or pork cutlet coated in egg and breadcrumbs then sautéed in butter.
Wiener Backhendl	Boned roast chicken prepared in the same way.
Tafelspitz	Boiled beef
Goulasch	Beef stewed in onions, garlic, paprika and tomatoes.
Geröstete	Sautéed potatoes.
Debrecziner	Spicy sausage
Schaschlik	Brochettes of lamb with onion, green and red peppers.
Cevapcici	Barbequed meatballs
Knödel	Dumplings
Marillenknödel	Dumplings with a hot apricot inside.
Topfenknödel	Dumplings of cream cheese
Palatschinken	Pancakes.
Apfelstrudel	Thinly sliced apple with raisins and cinnamon in flaky pastry.
Sachertorte	Viennese chocolate cake.

1.3 Your service in Central Europe

Changing Money

In all four countries, you can readily change money and travellers cheques at arrival airports, banks, exchange bureaux and larger hotels. You need to produce your passport. Commission rates vary and can be higher in hotels. Check first. Generally banks deduct a flat-rate minimum commission, making it uneconomic to change small sums of money.

Travellers Cheques

These are a safe way of carrying money but may be difficult to change at night or over the weekend, especially if you're travelling by surface routes to Prague or Budapest. It's best to arrive with a starter kit of Austrian Schillings or any other West-European hard currency to tide you over.

Credit cards

Plastic is generally accepted in Austria. Acceptance is more limited in Hungary, Poland and the Czech Republic, but there should be no problems with major cards in tourist areas of the main cities.

Eurocheques

Eurocheques are a safe and common method of payment. They can be obtained from your bank if ordered in advance. In Austria they are widely used in shops, restaurants etc when presented with a valid Eurocheque card. In Austria, numerous cash dispensers are open for use by cardholders. Look out for the blue and red 'ec' sticker.

Acceptance in shops is more limited in the Czech Republic, Poland and Hungary.

Currencies

The Austrian Schilling is almost identical to Britain's "old-fashioned" shilling – close to 20 to the pound. But you can't buy much for a Schilling! Austrian prices are somewhat higher than in Britain.

Coins are of 10 and 50 Groschen, and 1, 5, 10 and 20 Schillings. Banknotes are in denominations of 20, 50, 100, 200, 500, 1000 and 5000. The Schilling is usually abbreviated as Sch. or ÖS or AS or ATS.

(See sections 4.11, 5.11 and 6.7 for the Czech, Hungarian and Polish currencies).

Phoning home

Calls made from your hotel room are hassle-free; but most hotels at least double the cost onto your bill. To save money, try phoning from a street or Post Office call-box. Phone cards are the handiest choice.

For international calls dial 00 and wait for the tone to change; then dial country code (UK 44) + local area code minus the first 0; then the local number.

An audible tone will indicate that you need to insert more coins to continue your call.

Phoning from home

City dialling codes from UK are: 00 – then 43-1 for Vienna; 43-662 for Salzburg; 42-2 for Prague; 36-1 for Budapest; 48-22 for Warsaw; 48-12 for Kraków.

Dialling from USA or Canada: 011 – then codes as above.

Electricity

All four countries are on 220 volts. Plugs are Continental-style two-pin. Pack a plug adaptor if you expect to use your own electric gadgets.

Central European Time

All four countries are on basic GMT plus one hour – the same time zone as most of Western Europe. So Britain is usually one hour behind, but also gets out of step through choosing different dates to switch between summer and winter times. Take care when adjusting your watch in late March and September/October! Central European time is normally 6 hours ahead of Eastern Standard time.

Medical

Should you see a doctor while on holiday, you will have to pay for the consultation. If you intend to claim an insurance refund, get a receipt both from the doctor and the chemist. If sizeable funds are required to cover medical expenses, contact your tour rep for advice.

Tipping

If some Austrian menu prices make you whistle, they usually include all the obligatory extras such as 10% drinking tax, 10% alcohol tax, 15% service charge, and 10 or 20% VAT. In restaurants, just round off the bill. When service is not included, a 10% tip is normal.

Austrian National Tourist Offices

More information is available from these addresses:

30 St. George Street, London W1R 0AL. Tel: 0171-629 0461.

500 Fifth Ave, Suite 2009-2022, New York NY 10110. Tel: (212)-944 6880. Offices also in Chicago, Houston and Los Angeles.

2 Bloor Street East, Suite 3330, Toronto, Ontario M4W 1A8. Tel: (416)-967 3348.

News

In Austria, the regular broadsheet newspapers from London, such as *Daily Telegraph* cost AS 35, but *The Guardian* – printed in Frankfurt – is cheaper and arrives earlier than papers from UK. That also applies in Prague and Budapest. In Poland, English newspapers are harder to find.

Chapter Two

Vienna

2.1 Waltz in to Vienna

Vienna conjures up visions of a never-never musical comedy city of moonlight on the Blue Danube, and of waltzing through the Vienna Woods.

Of course it's difficult for any city to live up to such sugar-coated expectations. The days of an elegant nobility, splendid in fancy-dress uniform, ended over 70 years ago with collapse of the Austro-Hungarian empire.

Yet there is still much elegance and charm in the Viennese way of life. Down Vienna's most fashionable streets – Kohlmarkt, Graben and Kärntner-Strasse – shops can rival the most expensive streets of Paris, Rome or London.

In famous pastry-shops and coffeehouses, the smartly-dressed clientele savours the greatest luxury of all: a leisured indifference to the passing of time.

The Viennese pride themselves on their mastery of the art of living. They enjoy a highly civilised tradition.

The setting favours the old-fashioned civilities. Much of central Vienna looks like a collection of historic stage sets, but well-kept and newly painted. The Vienna of the Habsburg Empire still dominates the architectural scene.

In late 19th century, medieval walls surrounding the inner city were removed by order of Emperor Franz Josef. In their place, the Ring-Strasse was laid out - a broad, tree-lined series of boulevards encircling the old city, with pleasant parks, squares and sedate public buildings every few hundred yards.

The buildings were solid, meant to endure for evermore. The basic layout remains unchanged. Vienna has not yielded to the postwar passion for ripping down the old and rebuilding with skyscrapers. A citizen of the 1890's would not be lost in the central Vienna of today.

Winter and summer palaces of the Habsburgs still call up memories of when Austria was a great power. Schönbrunn Palace, summer residence of the Emperors, was one of Europe's finest royal homes, with 1441 rooms and 139 kitchens.

VIENNA

Royal art

For the history-minded visitor, Vienna has numerous such palaces and monuments to offer. But the art-lover has an even better time. For centuries, the Habsburg monarchs collected masterpieces from every school of painting.

Their taste was broad. Some members of the Imperial family preferred the Venetian Renaissance and bought a few dozen Titians and Tintorettos; others liked the Flemish masters, especially Brueghel and Rubens, or cornered the market in Italian primitives.

The buying continued steadily, from Middle Ages until 1918. With folding of the Austro-Hungarian monarchy, the Austrian State took over the collection - one of the world's greatest, rivalled only by the Prado, Louvre and Vatican. Vienna's Art History Museum could keep any art connoisseur delighted for weeks.

Other travellers prefer to make the musician's pilgrimage: visiting places associated with the numerous composers who made Vienna their home.

If pressed for time, that pilgrimage can be settled in one sightseeing stop, by dining at the Griechenbeisl Inn, the oldest eating-house in Vienna.

Established in 15th century, the Griechenbeisel has been the meeting-place for artists, composers and scientists ever since. The walls and low ceiling of one dining-room are entirely covered with reproduced signatures of the famous: Beethoven, Haydn, Schubert, Strauss, Brahms, Chaliapin...

Vienna still keeps its reputation as a world capital of classical and light music. A performance at the State Opera House is among the great musical memories of a lifetime. If you're aiming for the musical highlights, time your visit carefully. During summer season the State Opera closes, and the focal-point of classical music moves to Salzburg, for the annual Salzburg Festival.

2.2 Arrival & Hotels

From Britain direct flights to Vienna are operated by British Airways, Austrian Airlines and Lauda-Air.

At the arrival, airport trolleys can be unleashed only with an Austrian coin. An exchange office in the baggage hall can split a note.

From the International Airport at Schwechat, there are two bus services: to the City Air Terminal at Hotel Hilton beside the Stadtpark; and to the South and West Railway Stations. Cost: AS 70.

The 11-mile journey to the city centre takes between 20 and 30 minutes. The highway follows the old Roman road into Vienna, parallel with the Danube Canal and passing through a light industrial zone where the most popular product is beer. En route there's a golf course, which is also used for trotting races.

In the following list are the most important sites in the central area, marked on the orientation map overleaf.

Clockwise around the Ring

1	State Opera House
2	Academy of Fine Arts
3	Secession – "the golden cabbage"
4	Art History Museum
5	Imperial Palace Gates, Heldenplatz & Neue Burg museums
6	Maria Theresa monument
7	Museum quarter
8	Natural History Museum
9	Palace of Justice
10	Parliament
11	Burgtheater – National Theatre
12	Rathaus – City Hall
13	University of Vienna
14	Votive Church & Sigmund Freud Park
15	Börse – Stock Exchange
16	Schwedenbrücke – for Danube boats
17	former Imperial Defence Ministry
18	Musem of Applied Art
19	City Air Terminal
20	Johann Strauss monument
21	Vienna Concert House
22	Soviet War Memorial
23	Vienna Philharmonic Musikverein
24	Vienna City Museum
25	Church of St Charles Borromeo
26	Stadtbahn art nouveau Pavilions
27	Technical University buildings
28	Produce market & Saturday flea market

Inside the Ring

29	Albertina; Augustinian Friars Church
30	Imperial Burial Vault, Capuchin Church
31	Imperial Palace, State Rooms, Chapel
32	Spanish Riding School
33	St Michael's Sq; Excavations
34	Chancellor's office
35	Our Lady's Column & Am Hof church
36	Old City Hall
37	"Anker" Clock; St Joseph's Column
38	St Stephen's Cathedral
39	Palace of the Archbishops
40	Plague Column
41	Mozart memorial
42	Franziskaner Platz – Franciscan Church

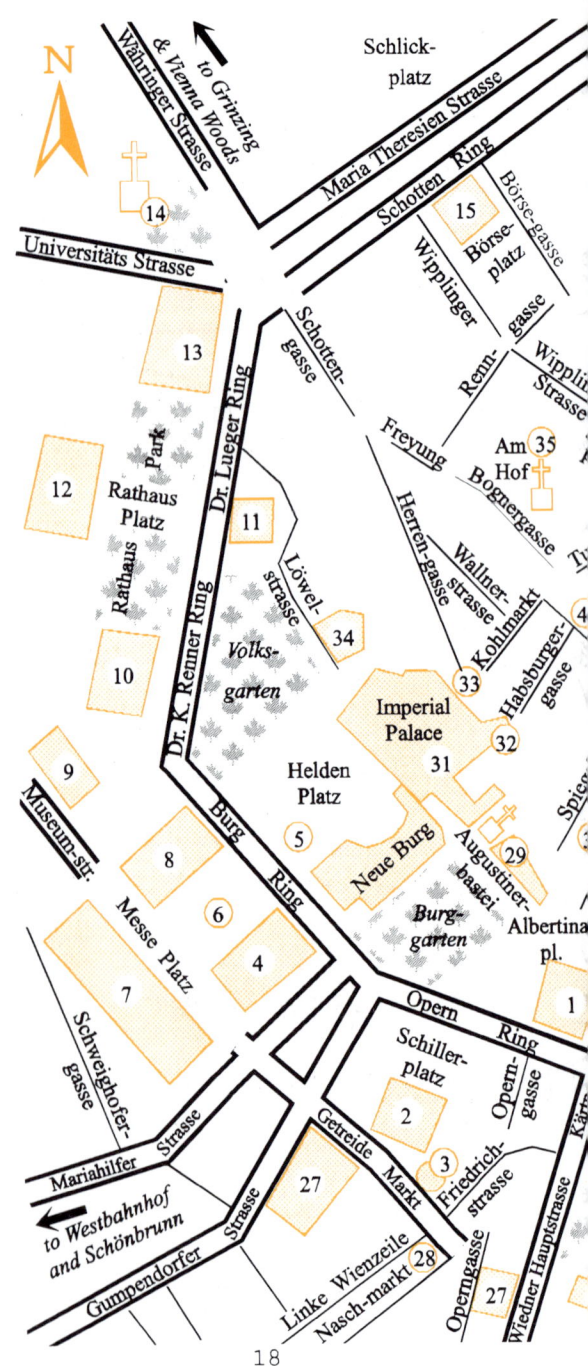

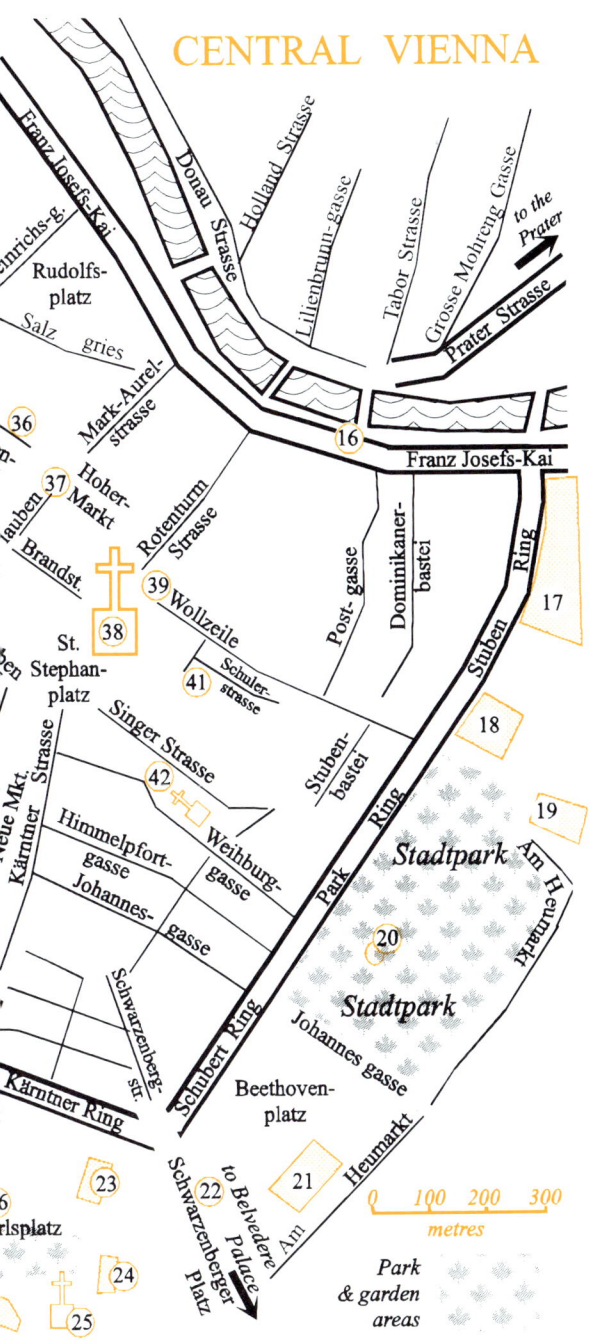

CENTRAL VIENNA

Franz Josefs-Kai

enrichs-g.

Rudolfs-platz

Salz gries

Holland Strasse

Donau Strasse

Lilienbrunn-gasse

Tabor Strasse

Grosse Mohreng Gasse

to the Prater

Prater Strasse

Mark-Aurel-strasse

36

lauben-

37 Hoher-Markt

Brandst

Rotenturm Strasse

Franz Josefs-Kai

16

Post-gasse

Dominikaner-bastei

Stuben Ring

17

39 Wollzeile

St. Stephan-platz

38

en

41 Schuler-strasse

Stuben-bastei

18

Singer Strasse

42

Weihburg-gasse

Park Ring

Stadtpark

19

Am Heumarkt

Neue Mkt.

Kärntner Strasse

Himmelpfort-gasse

Johannes-gasse

20

Stadtpark

Schwarzenberg-str.

Schubert Ring

Johannes gasse

Kärntner Ring

Beethoven-platz

Heumarkt

23

22

to Belvedere

Schwarzenberger Platz

21

Am

0   100   200   300
metres

rlsplatz

24

6

Park & garden areas

25

19

VIENNA

Airport taxi

A taxi to or from the airport will cost about AS 500, plus AS 15 for each piece of luggage in the boot. On departure from your hotel, it's worth asking about a lower-cost transfer by minibus.

Hotels

Vienna's peak seasons are New Year, Easter, May, June, September, October and Christmas. Lower hotel tariffs are offered from November through March. The most sought-after hotels are those in the First District – inside the Ring – or on the Ring itself or very close. From these hotels, most of the sightseeing, shopping, restaurants, cafés and nightlife is within walking distance.

For non-central hotels, guests have frequent tram, bus or subway services to the inner city.

2.3 Get your bearings

The original heart of Vienna was surrounded by a massive Ring of fortress walls and bastions which were removed in the 1850's. In their place the Ringstrasse was laid out – a broad tree-lined circle of boulevards, three miles of splendid parks and public buildings on either side. The pattern and style of Vienna today is governed by the Ring, with the Danube Canal shaping the northeastern segment. *See map on previous page.*

Thus the Ring encircles District 1, the Inner Town which has kept its historic layout, and many of its original buildings. Most of the classic sightseeing highlights are located within the Ring, while the 19th century is represented *on* the Ring in a belt 300 metres wide.

Further out from the Ring is another concentric circle of boulevards called the Gürtel – the Girdle or Belt. This encloses Districts 2 to 9, which are helpfully numbered in a clockwise direction.

District 2, called Leopolds-Stadt, is wedged between the Danube Canal and the present line of the Danube River itself. Beyond the Gürtel are Districts 10 to 23, which form the suburbs. On the western outskirts are the hills of the Vienna Woods.

Every street-name in Vienna is painted with its District number, to ease the problem of finding where you are. In this book, all addresses outside the Inner City are given with their District number.

Public transport

At the start of your visit, it's worth taking a little time to crack the Viennese transport system, based on an excellent network of trams, buses and subways. Tram No. 1 goes round and round the Ring, clockwise; No. 2 goes anti-clockwise. Subway Line U2 does a half-circle around the Ring, from Karlsplatz (south of the Opera House), to Schottenring (by the Danube Canal). Subway lines U1 and U3 cross within the Ring, and can take you dead central to Stephansplatz – one of the best starting points for exploring the old city. *See map fig. 38.*

Rover tickets

Most other tram, bus and subway services feed into the Ring, and radiate to the suburbs. *Inside* the Ring there's virtually no public transport, except for three city buses which circulate; and the subway stop at Stefansplatz. Much of the Inner City is pedestrianized, and most sites are within a five-minute walk of a tram or subway stop on the Ring.

A single-ride ticket costing AS 20 is good for one trip in one direction, including transfers. But most people use advance-purchased tickets which are more economical. A single ticket then costs AS 17. On a City Break the best deal is a 72-hour pass for unlimited travel on trams, buses, underground (U-Bahn) and city trains within the central zone. Cost is AS 130. Timing of the 72 hours starts from date-stamping on the first ride.

An alternative is a 24-hour pass costing AS 50.

Another excellent deal is the Vienna Card, combining the 72-hour transport pass with discounts for museums etc.

These various tickets are sold at tobacconists' shops, marked by a sign "Austria Tabak" in white letters on a red circle, held outstretched by a metal filter-tip cigarette. The tickets are also available at the Transport Information Offices at Karlsplatz or Stefanplatz.

Anyone who wants to make more serious use of the Vienna transport system should buy the excellent network map for buses, trams and subways published by the transport authority, price AS 15. All tram stops are clearly named, helping you chart your route.

To validate your ticket with date and time, stamp it in a blue box called an Entwerter either at the subway barrier, or at the middle or back of trams and buses. Normally there are no conductors. To get off, press the button by the exit doors. Travel without a valid ticket costs AS 520.

During Vienna's school holidays at Easter, Whitsun and Summer (all July-August), foreign children under 16 years can travel free, but should carry passport as proof.

Taxis

Cab ranks can be found at busy locations and can also be hailed in the street – though whether or not they'll stop is another matter. Watch for the illuminated sign "Frei".

Taxis are costly. The fare is shown by an official meter plus a few Schillings surcharge for inflation. Luggage in the boot costs an extra 10 to 15 Schillngs per piece. For a radio cab dial 60160 or 40100, with an AS 16 surcharge.

VIENNA

Fiaker (Horse-Carriage) Rides

The old-time Viennese "Fiaker" are flourishing. They clip-clop around the city on sightseeing circuits. Most drivers wear the traditional costume of Pepita trousers, velvet jacket and a hat rather like a bowler, called a "Stosser". It's a leisured and stylish way of seeing the sights, but pricey!

Four-passenger Fiakers can be hired at these locations: Stephansplatz; Albertina Platz (behind Opera House – *see map fig. 1*); Heldenplatz (by the Hofburg – *map fig. 5*).

Settle the price before starting. Reckon something like AS 400 for 20 mins; AS 500 for 30 minutes; AS 800 for 40 minutes.

Bicycles

Vienna is well provided with cycle paths. One can cycle throughout the central areas and beside the Danube waterways without having to jostle with motorised traffic. A typical rental price starts at AS 40 an hour.

The Tourist Information Office gives out a pamphlet showing cycle routes and addresses of bike-hire firms.

2.4 Basic Vienna

Give yourself six months, and you can see everything in Vienna. Otherwise, on a short city break, at least try to cover the essentials:

(1) Get your bearings with the standard City Sightseeing tour, including Schönbrunn Palace to see how the Habsburgs lived.

(2) Go shop-gazing along Kärntnerstrasse, Graben and Kohlmarkt.

(3) Relax with coffee and Sachertorte at Sacher's or Demel's, and hang the expense.

(4) Try to get tickets for the State Opera. If no luck, take the daytime tour back-stage or console yourself with the Volksoper. *See map fig. 1.*

(5) Have an evening Heuriger tavern-crawl at Grinzing, getting merry on new wine.

(6) Check the colour rating of the Blue Danube by taking a cruise. *Departure point, fig. 16 on map.*

(7) Visit the Art History Museum to see one of the world's greatest collections. *See map fig. 4.*

(8) Schedule a Vienna Woods tour, to include Heiligenkreuz Monastery and the hunting lodge at Mayerling.

(9) At noon, watch the performance of the Anker Clock in Hoher Markt for a 12-minute potted history of Vienna with organ music. *See map fig. 37.*

(10) Wallow in Johann Strauss nostalgia during the evening show at the Kursalon in the Stadtpark, and enjoy watching Japanese tourists doing the waltz.

Orientation

The introductory city tour helps you get your bearings, with a circuit of the Ring, into the city centre by the Cathedral, a drive across the Danube Canal to the River; and then to the Palace of Schönbrunn, with a guided tour of the apartments, and time to stroll in the Palace park.

Let's follow the standard city tour routing for leisured sightseeing and photography under your own steam.

Note that museum entry times and prices are for guidance, and may change. Many entrances are greatly reduced for children, students and senior citizens. Best buy is the 'Vienna Card' which includes the 72-hour transport pass and discount entry prices.

Clockwise around the Ring

Starting from the State Opera House, you can walk right round the three miles of the Ring; or take Tram No. 1 (clockwise) and get off anywhere you want to look closer. To reverse the itinerary – anti-clockwise – take Tram No. 2.

All the major monuments along the route are about 120 years old, copies of traditional architectural styles from classical Greek onwards. After dark, most of the buildings and monuments are illuminated.

Opera House – Staatsoper

In 1869, this was the Ring's first building to be completed. It opened to Mozart's *Don Giovanni*. Built in French Renaissance style, the Staatsoper ranks among the world's three leading opera houses, home to the Vienna State Opera. *See map fig. 1.*

It's an enormous building with audience capacity of 2200. When all lights are switched on, the Staatsoper consumes enough electricity for a city of 40,000. The season of 300 performances runs from September 1 through June 30. Eighty per cent of costs are met by government subsidy.

See chapter 2.10 for ticket-buying strategy.

For AS 60 you can have a 45-minute English-speaking backstage tour, most days at 1, 2 and 3 p.m. Check timings, as sometimes tours are cancelled for reheasals. During the afternoon, scene-shifters are busy preparing the stage for the first act of that evening's performance; so access to the stage is less possible.

The Opera House is one of Vienna's major focal points, with a shop-lined underpass leading to the nearest U-Bahn station of Karlsplatz.

Alongside runs the principal axis of the Inner City, the Kärntner Strasse, a pedestrian shopping precinct through to St. Stephen's Cathedral.

Behind the Opera House is Hotel Sacher on Philharmoniker Strasse, which leads to Albertina Platz where horse-carriages wait for passengers.

Burggarten

Clockwise round the Ring, there's a monument to the poet Schiller on the left, backed by the **Academy of Fine Arts**. Then, at the corner of the Burggarten (right), Goethe is slumped in an armchair.

Formerly, these Gardens of the Imperial Palace were for court use only. The Burggarten has been a public park since 1918, a popular spot for picnics. Sited amid the trees is the Mozart Memorial, one of Vienna's most delightful monuments, with foreground flower beds in the shape of a treble clef.

Art History Museum – Kunsthistorisches Museum

Next (right) is entrance to the Hofburg – the Winter Palace: see later in this chapter. Opposite (left) is a stately trio of buildings around Maria-Theresien Platz. *See map fig. 6.* Identical-twin museums in Italian Renaissance style face each other across the small park: Art History and Natural History. *See map figs. 4 and 8.*

Closing off the square in the background is the huge Trade Fair Palace – Messepalast – which originally was built in 1725 to house the Imperial coaches and horses. *See map fig. 7.* Central in the park is a monument to Empress Maria Theresa, sitting loftily on her throne with generals, statesmen and musicians at her feet.

The Art History Museum is among the richest in the world, and is particularly famous for galleries of Rubens, Dürer, Brueghel and Italian Schools. The Museum was purpose-built in 1881 to house this magnificent collection, formed by a succession of art-loving kings and emperors who each bought or inherited more treasures.

Quite outstanding is the gallery devoted to Pieter Brueghel the Elder. Nowhere else are so many of his paintings grouped together: comic masterpieces, alive with every detail of Flemish peasant life.

Paintings are located on the first floor, up a monumental staircase dominated by a marble group by Canova – *Theseus and the Centaur*. At mezzanine level, among Sculpture and Minor Arts, is the famed golden salt cellar by Benvenuto Cellini.

Even without the art-work, the interior of the building is a fantasy. Give your feet a rest in the central coffee bar on the first floor, and absorb the atmosphere.

Open: Tue-Sun 10-18 hrs, but Tue and Fri until 21 hrs. Entrance AS 45.

Volksgarten

The "Peoples' Garden" (right) is the second largest park in the city centre. It's renowned for beautiful rose gardens and is a favourite choice for a Viennese Sunday afternoon stroll. Look for the imitation Greek temple built 1825, and a memorial to Franz Josef's wife Empress Elizabeth.

Parliament

Next building (*fig. 10*) is Parliament, facing the Volksgarten. In neo-Greek style, it is garnished with imitation Greek statues, symbolic of democracy. Pallas Athena – goddess of wisdom – presides over the fountain outside. The guides say there's no room for her within.

National Theatre – Burgtheater

Past the Volksgarten is Café Landtmann (right) – one of the four traditional coffeehouses that still remain on the Ring. Formerly there were 36.

The green-roofed building is the National Theatre (*fig. 11*), built 1888. The original Court and National Theatre was formed in 1776, and was among the most important and influential theatres in German-speaking Europe.

Backstage tours are available on varying days according to season. Cost is AS 60. Check timings by phone 51444.

City Hall – Rathaus

Facing the Burgtheater is City Hall (*fig. 12*), an impressive neo-Gothic building topped by an 11-ft knight who is the city's "iron man", a symbol of Vienna. The pattern for the Rathaus was the Town Hall of Brussels.

During summer nights, concerts are held in the Arcaded Courtyard; and opera films are shown on the Square outside, free. The attractive City Hall Park includes statues of two waltz composers: Joseph Lanner and Johann Strauss Senior.

University

On the left is the University building (*fig. 13*), completed in Italian Renaissance style in 1884. Vienna University is the oldest in German-speaking Europe, established 1365. Currently Vienna's student population is around 90,000.

Votive Church

Next (left) rises the neo-Gothic Votive Church (*fig. 14*), built in thanksgiving for Emperor Franz Josef's survival from an assassination attempt. In front is Sigmund Freud Park, named after the psychologist who lived close by.

Danube Canal

Along Schottenring the building resembling an Italian palace (right) is the Stock Exchange, built 1877. Finally the Ring reaches the Danube Canal, and turns along Franz Josef Kai (Quay). This is *not* the waterfront of the main river, which has been straightened and rechanneled as a flood-control policy. Schwedenbrücke is departure point for local sightseeing cruises. The paddle steamer *Johann Strauss* is permanently moored close by as a floating café and music pavilion. *See map fig. 16.*

Stubenring

The tram route turns away from the Canal, into Stuben-
ring, to continue the circle. The former Imperial Defence
Ministry with a monument to Field Marshall Radetzky
(left) is used as government offices. Radetzky well de-
served a monument, being active in the Imperial Army
for 72 years. *See map fig. 17.*

The next block (left) is the red-brick **Academy of
Applied Art**, a miniature edition of London's Victoria
and Albert. Founded 1864, this museum has good collections of porcelain, glass and period furniture. An entire
hall is devoted to Art Nouveau, which flourished in turn-
of-the-century Vienna. *See map fig. 18.*

Open: Daily except Mon, 10-18 hrs; on Thursday until
21 hrs. Entrance AS 30.

Stadtpark – City Park

Covering 22 acres – largest of Vienna's 800 parks –
these landscaped gardens were opened in 1862. Charming
little bridges cross the Wien River, Vienna's tributary to
the Danube. The Stadtpark features monuments to Viennese musicians, including Schubert, Bruckner and Lehar.

Top favourite is a memorial to Johann Strauss, whose
statue makes a romantic subject for every passing camera. *See map fig. 20.* His role as king of the waltz is still
honoured daily at the Kursalon, where one-hour open-air
Strauss concerts are given every fine afternoon from
Easter till late October; and also every evening indoors.
A waltz show is given daily from 20.30 hrs, costing
from AS 390 to 550 including a drink.

Several major luxury hotels are located in this area –
Hilton and Inter-Continental facing one another from
opposite ends of the Stadtpark; and Vienna Marriott and
SAS Palais Hotel along the Ring.

Schwarzenberg Platz and Kärntner Ring

Left is a square dominated by a monument to Field-Mar-
shall Schwarzenberg, who played a leading role in the
Napoleonic Wars. In the background is a Soviet memorial to men who died around Vienna in the last days of
World War II. *See map fig. 22.*

From Schwarzenberg Platz to the Opera House is
called Kärntner Ring. During the second half of the 19th
century, until the end of the monarchy, many of the
buildings were private homes of aristocratic families.
Mostly these have since been converted into hotels, banks
or travel bureaux.

Typically, the stately Imperial Hotel was originally a
private residence. The first floor apartment is completely
reserved for Very Important state guests. Hotel Bristol
almost opposite was the residence of a wealthy banker
from Prague. The Italian Tourist office was previously
the home of Emperor Franz Joseph's mistress.

Inner City – Inside the Ring

Hofburg – the Imperial Palace

Originally a medieval castle which grew wing by wing as Austrian power developed, this huge complex of palace buildings was the seat of the Habsburgs until 1918. *See map fig. 31.* Its size reflects the importance of Austria in the great days of the Austro-Hungarian empire. The palace was both the residence and the administrative centre of the Habsburg dynasty which ruled for over 600 years. Their golden age was the early 18th century, after the retreat of the Turks from the gates of Vienna.

Today the sprawling buildings house offices of the President and the Federal Chancellor; several museums, art galleries and state rooms open to the public; the Spanish Riding School; and the Court Chapel where the Vienna Boys' Choir sings Sunday mass.

Other parts of the complex are used as offices or private apartments. Thanks to its long history the Hofburg is an architectural assortment of Gothic, Renaissance, Baroque and Rococo.

There are several possible entrances. Let's start through the **Palace Gates** on the Ring, into **Heldenplatz** – Heroes Square. *See map fig. 5.* The Palace Gates themselves date from the Napoleonic war. On the right is a statue of Prince Eugene of Savoy, who defeated the Turks; left is Archduke Charles who vanquished Napoleon in 1809. In 1938, when Hitler annexed Austria, a giant triumphal rally was held in this square.

Face towards the main palace, and the President's quarters are to the left. Keep looking round anti-clockwise, and you get a dramatic skyline view of major buildings on the Ring: National Theatre, City Hall, Parliament and back to the Museums of Natural History and Art History.

Neue Burg

On your right beyond Prince Eugene is the curved facade of the Neue Burg – the New Palace – completed in 1913 as an ambitious extension to the main premises. Two museums now occupy the building: Ethnological and Ephesus. The latter museum incorporates turn-of-the-century finds from Ephesus in Turkey, where the Austrian school of archaeology continues to dig.

Also on view are collections of Arms – ranking second largest in the world – and of Historical Musical Instruments. (Open daily except Tuesday till 18 hrs. Entrance AS 30, but due to be increased.)

Now walk straight on through the main archway into a courtyard with a monument to **Emperor Franz 11** (1792-1835). He was married four times, and although Napoleon besieged Vienna twice, he married off his daughter Marie-Louise to Napoleon.

State Rooms

Clockwise around the courtyard, start with **Amelia's Wing** built 1577, and distinguished by a 17th-century clock tower with a normal clock, a sundial, and a moon phase indicator.

Next is the baroque-style **Imperial Chancery Wing** dated 1730, with apartments that are included in a guided sightseeing of the **State Rooms**, costing AS 80. The tour entrance is at St. Michael's Gate – reached by going straight ahead.

Facing the Imperial Chancery Wing is **Leopold's Wing** – the other side already seen from the Heldenplatz – where Maria Theresa's apartments are now used by the President.

A right turn brings you into the **Swiss Courtyard**, the oldest part of the original 13th-century fortified castle. The name comes from the Swiss mercenary guards who manned the gate. Here is public entrance to the **Treasuries** – Schatzkammer – containing the world's oldest collection of crown jewels, still complete and intact as they were by the 14th century.

The most prized possession is the 10th-century imperial crown of the Holy Roman Empire. (Open daily except Tuesday till 18 hrs. Entrance AS 80.)

Vienna Boys' Choir

From the courtyard a staircase leads to the entrance of the mid-15th century Gothic-style **Chapel** – the Burgkapelle – where the Vienna Boys' Choir performs. (For admission to High Mass see section 2.7 'Sunday in Vienna').

More archways lead out of the Hofburg into Josefsplatz, with a central monument to **Emperor Joseph 11** (1780-1790), who was a son of Maria Theresa. He was a great reformer, and tried to improve the poor standard of living of the farmers. His grandfather built the beautiful **National Library**, which faces the monument. The facade is typical Baroque, the roof modern.

The Spanish Riding School, 2 Reitschulgasse

A wing of the Hofburg leads off from Josefsplatz and goes along Reitschulgasse into Michaelerplatz. *See map fig. 32.* Built in mid-16th century, the wing was later converted into stables for the white Lippizaner horses of the Spanish Riding School, which was founded in 1572.

The world-famed performances are given in traditional costume. Riders wear buckskin breeches and bicorn hats trimmed with gold. Deerskin saddles lie over the horses' gold-trimmed red and blue saddle cloths. The School is closed throughout July and most of August.

Morning training sessions are normally open to the public from late February until the end of June; late August till mid-October; and in the first half of December. They are held Tue-Fri from 10-12 hrs.

Getting tickets

To get a seat, rather than standing, start queuing not later than 9.30. During chilly weather, it's really cold inside! Tickets are sold at the entrance – no reservations – and cost AS 100 for adults, AS 30 for children.

There is training with music on some Saturday mornings, starting at 10 hrs, entrance AS 250.

Full-dress performances lasting 80 minutes are mostly on Sunday morning, starting at 10.45 hrs; or on some Wednesdays at 19 hrs. Entry is only with pre-booked tickets that cost from AS 250 to 900 for seats; standing room AS 200. Ticket and travel agencies charge at least an additional 22%.

Written orders can be sent direct to Spanische Reit-schule, Hofburg, A-1010 Vienna. Do not enclose money! You can order by fax: +43-1-5350186. Ticket and travel agencies can also obtain tickets, but most unlikely at short notice.

Dates of performances and training sessions are subject to change, so check the programmes. A number of city sightseeing tours include a Spanish Riding School visit, with entrance tickets paid separately on the tour coach.

St. Stephen's Cathedral

In the heart of the Inner City stands Vienna's most important Gothic building. St. Stephen's Cathedral, with its 450-ft spire, and roof covered by 250,000 glazed tiles, is one of the capital's major landmarks. *See map fig. 38.*

Like most cathedrals which took centuries to build, St. Stephen's is a medley of architectural styles. The Giant Gate, and the Towers of the Heathens on either side of the entrance, are 12th-century Romanesque.

Then came a wave of building in Gothic style – the tall South Tower, for instance – followed by a short 16th-century North Tower topped by a Renaissance spire. The 18th century contributed Baroque altarpieces.

The North Tower houses the Boomer Bell – the Pummerin, the largest bell in Austria. The original was cast in early 18th century from captured Turkish cannons and was hung in the South Tower.

When the Cathedral was bombed and set alight in 1945, the Boomer fell and was shattered. The replacement – diameter 12 feet and weighing 21 tons – is rung on important church holidays only, and to usher in the New Year. That is one of Vienna's big public occasions, when the locals gather en masse to celebrate.

A lift can take you up the North Tower, price AS 40; or for AS 25 you can walk up 343 spiral stairs inside the South Tower to the dramatic viewpoint 246 feet above street level.

However, stay at ground level if you are nervous about heights! At the other extreme, in fact, the entrance to the catacombs is next to the North Tower lift.

Stephansplatz

Stand with your back to the main entrance of St. Stephen's Cathedral. Here is the crossing point of the Inner City's main routes. To get your bearings: Kärntner Strasse is to your left; Rotenturm Strasse right; Graben straight ahead; Singer Strasse behind the Cathedral. Wander along each of those axes and their side turnings, to make a myriad personal discoveries of Old Vienna. The route permutations are endless!

Kärntner Strasse is the Inner City's most famous shopping street, named after the province of Carinthia (Kärntnen), which borders Italy. No. 41 is Esterhazy Palace, with an apartment still used by the family. But mainly it's a Casino, open daily from 3 p.m., with a fashion salon below. Kärntner Strasse virtually dives below the Ring at the Opera House – a lengthy pedestrian and shopping underpass called Opernpassage – to end at Karlsplatz.

Along **Rotenturm Strasse**, the first building on the right is the Archbishop's Palace, built 1640. *See map fig. 39.* A left turning called Lichtensteg brings you to Hoher Markt with its Anker Clock (see below). Streets to the right lead to a good area for shops and restaurants (see section 2.9). Further down Rotenturm Strasse at Fleischmarkt leads to other suggested restaurant areas – the Bermuda Triangle veering to the left; the Greek Orthodox Church and the Griechenbeisl Inn to the right.

The **Graben**, its side streets and Kohlmarkt are at the high end of shopping elegance and price. This area was the southern side of a Roman fortress without a natural line of defence. So Roman soldiers had to fortify their camp by hand, and dug a protective moat – for which the German word is Graben. *See map fig. 40.*

Centred in the Graben is the **Plague Column,** a wildly ornate 17th century memorial erected in thanksgiving for final deliverance from the black plague of 1679. On the other side is a monument to Saint Christopher, patron saint of travellers. Underneath is a WC from the Art Nouveau period, now one of Vienna's tourist attractions.

In the other direction, **Singer Strasse** leads to **Franziskaner Platz** – one of the most attractive old squares in Vienna with its Franciscan monastery and church, and 17th and 18th century buildings. *See map fig. 42.* Further along brings you to the Stadtpark.

Anker Clock

For an entertaining 12 minutes, go to the Hoher Markt just before noon. The Anker Insurance Company erected this decorative clock in 1911. *See map fig. 37.*

At midday a dozen historic figures or pairs of figures parade slowly across the clock face, with appropriate background music – from Emperor Marcus Aurelius of Roman times through to Joseph Haydn.

Outside the Ring

Karlsplatz

A few minutes' walk from the Opera House, Karlsplatz is an interesting transport focal-point, where three subway lines – U1, U2 and U4 – intersect. Vienna's underground rail system dates from 1900, when Art Nouveau was "in". *See map fig. 26.*

Chief architect for the project was Otto Wagner, who introduced Art Nouveau ideas into every detail of construction. Several of his station buildings have been restored along line U4 – Rossauer Länder, Stadtpark, Karlsplatz, Kettenbrückengasse and Schönbrunn – a good tourist line!

The Karlsplatz entrance pavilion is a delight, and well worth a picture or two. The setting is charming, in Ressel Park which is surrounded by stately buildings. On the corner of Dumbastrasse is the **Musikverein** – the 'Music Society' which is home of the Vienna Philharmonic. Its annual New Year's Day concert is always broadcast around the world. *See map fig. 23.*

Clockwise, the next building around the park is the **Historical Museum of the City of Vienna**, which can help give deeper understanding to your sightseeing. With pictures, maps etc it surveys Vienna from early times to the present. (Open: daily except Monday, 9-16.30 hrs. Entrance AS 50.) *See map fig. 24.*

Karlskirche

Then – impossible to miss with its distinctive green roof – comes the **Church of St. Charles Borromeo (Karlskirche)**, which ranks as Vienna's finest baroque church. *See map fig. 25.* A masterpiece of the architect Fischer von Erlach, the church was completed in 1737. The foreground pool and the two spiral columns combine with the elegant facade to make a most unusual monument. Inside, paintings are by Michael Rottmayr.

In front of the church, a reflecting pool features a Henry Moore sculpture which gives foreground interest for photographers. Further round the edge of the park are buildings of the Technical University. *See map fig. 27.*

Art Nouveau

Follow through to the end of the park, to reach the white cube-shaped **Secession** gallery topped by an ornate golden cabbage. It's dedicated to Art Nouveau, with a famed Beethoven Frieze representing the 9th Symphony on permanent display in the basement. At the entrance counters are publications and prints that cover every aspect of the Art Nouveau era. (Open Tue-Fri 10-18 hrs; Sat-Sun 10-16 hrs.) *See map fig. 3.*

Finally – get your bearings – you are now close to Naschmarkt, *(fig. 28),* the daily retail food market which leads to the Saturday flea market. (See section 2.8.)

Schönbrunn Palace

This splendid summer residence of the Habsburgs was built between 1696 and 1713, designed by the master architect of Viennese Baroque, Fischer von Erlach. The principal State Rooms in best Rococo style are open to the public on guided tours. A visit is normally included on standard city sightseeings.

One of the great highlights of Vienna, the fabulous Room of Millions is still used for major state receptions. The first royal tenant was Empress Maria Theresa, who helped populate the 1441 rooms of the palace by producing 16 children. Emperor Franz Josef was the longest-living of the royal residents, born here in 1830. He reigned from 1848 until his death in 1916.

Napoleon lodged here in 1805 and 1809, and his son died in the palace in 1832. In the Hall of Mirrors, Mozart performed at age six.

The adjoining park covers about 500 acres with formal gardens, fountains, vistas and severely trimmed hedges and ruler-straight avenues in the accepted style of Baroque landscape gardening. The park is open daily, free, from 6 a.m. till dusk.

The Imperial Coach Collection is located in the right wing of the palace, near the main entrance gate. (Open Tue-Sun 10-17 hrs May-Sep; 10-16 hrs Oct-April. Entrance AS 30.)

Belvedere Palace

This two-section palace – an Upper and a Lower Belvedere (Oberes and Unteres) – is regarded as Vienna's most splendid example of residential Baroque architecture. The garden setting is stately, offering a superb view across central Vienna to background hills of the Vienna Woods.

Built by Prince Eugene of Savoy in a wine-growing area outside the city walls, Lower Belvedere was his summer residence, while Upper Belvedere was designed for banquets and other festivities.

Besides being very rich, Prinz Eugene was a brilliant general who defeated the Turks 17 times in battle. After Prinz Eugen's death, the Palace was acquired by the Habsburg family.

Among later residents of the Belvedere was Archduke Ferdinand, whose assassination in Sarajevo sparked the First World War.

The Lower Belvedere (entrance on Rennweg – Tram F1 or O) and its Orangery house collections of Medieval Austrian Art, and a Baroque Museum.

The Upper Belvedere (entrance on Prinz Eugen Strasse – Tram D) features 19th- and 20th-century Austrian art through to modern times, including a major collection of Art Nouveau.

Open: Tue-Sun 10-16 hrs. Entrance AS 60. No charge for admission to the grounds.

2.5 Other sights in Vienna

Depending on your personal interests and time available, here are some suggestions for supplementary sightseeing.

Capuchin Church & Imperial Vault, Neuer Markt
Close to Kärntnerstrasse, the Capuchin Church is very modest, with little ornamentation. *See map fig. 30.* The Imperial Vault houses the remains of 139 members of the Habsburg family. Open Apr-Sep 10-18 hrs. Entry AS 40.

Museum of Natural History, Maria Theresein Platz
A fascinating collection of Natural History exhibited in 39 galleries and a domed hall. *See map fig. 8.*
Open: daily except Tue 9-18 hrs. Entrance AS 30.

Sigmund Freud's House, Berggasse 19
This house, faithfully reconstructed and with some original furniture, is a Mecca for students of psychoanalysis. Freud lived here from 1891 until 1938 when the Nazis arrived. His couch is in London. *See map near fig. 14.*
Open: Daily 9-16 hrs. Located in District 9, near the Votive Church (U-Bahn Schottentor). Entrance AS 60.

Jewish Museum, Palais Eskeles, Dorotheergasse 11
Focusses on the cultural history of Jewish Vienna, with a series of limited-run exhibitions.
Open: Sun-Fri 10-18 hrs, Thu until 21 hrs. Entry AS 70.

Museum of Military History
In the Armory on Arsenalstrasse, District 3, are valuable collections related to weapons and warfare in Austria, from the Thirty Years' War to the First World War. In the Sarajevo Room, see the bloodstained uniform of Archduke Franz Ferdinand.
Open: Daily except Fri 10-16 hrs. Entrance AS 40.
Near South Station (Südbahnhof). Trams: D, 18.

Special for art-lovers
Vienna offers great riches in art masterpieces through the ages, with the Art History Museum as the great treasure-house. The city has also been in the forefront of 20th-century creative activity from Art Nouveau onwards. Check the month's programme for details of special exhibitions in the city's numerous galleries.

Academy of Fine Arts, Schillerplatz
On the south side of the Ring, facing towards Opera House and the Burggarten, this impressive picture gallery is rich in 17th-century Dutch and Flemish paintings, especially Rubens. *See map fig. 2.*
Open: Tue-Sun 10-18 hrs; Tue and Fri until 21 hrs. Entrance AS 30. U-Bahn: Karlsplatz.

Albertina Collection of Graphic Arts, Augustinerstrasse
Just behind the Opera House, a fabulous collection of
graphic material – drawings, watercolours, etchings and
prints by many famous artists including Raphael, Dürer,
Leonardo da Vinci, Michelangelo, Rubens and Rembrandt. The world's largest collection of 1.5 million
prints covers the art of printmaking since it began in the
15th century. A must! *See map fig. 29.*
Open: Mon, Tue, Thur 10-16 hrs; Wed 10-18 hrs; Fri
10-14 hrs; Sat & Sun 10-13 hrs. July/Aug closed Sundays. Entrance AS 45.

Museum of Modern Art, Liechtenstein Palace, 9
Fürstengasse 1
Devoted to works by 20th-century artists including
Derain, Ernst, Kirchner, Picasso, Warhol.
Open: Daily except Tue 10-18 hrs. Entrance AS 45.
In 9th District along Porzellangasse, Tram D stops out-
side.

Museum of the 20th Century, Schweizergarten
A branch of the Modern Art Museum, features special
exhibitions of contemporary art. On permanent display in
the statuary garden are modern sculptures including
works by Giacometti and Henry Moore.
Open; Daily except Wed 12-18 hrs. Entrance AS 30.
In 3rd District, by South Station (Südbahnhof). Trams:
D, 18.

The musical pilgrimage

Vienna is supremely rich in memories of the many composers who lived here. Numerous apartments, preserved
as small museums, can be visited. The most famous and
convenient is the Figaro House on Domgasse – two minutes from the Cathedral – where Mozart composed *The
Marriage of Figaro.* If time is scarce, this could serve as
your homage to classical music. 1999 is Johann Strauss
Year, the 100th anniversary of his death.

For something more in-depth, be prepared for widely
scattered visits throughout central Vienna and the suburbs. Beethoven, for instance, changed address twice
every year – in spring he moved to the country suburbs,
in autumn he returned to the centre.

An excellent guided coach tour visits a selection of
music-related locations in a half-day circuit, which otherwise would take much longer.

Mozart Memorial – "Figaro House", Domgasse 5
Mozart's one-floor apartment from 1784 to 1787. Smartly
decorated, and with a few items of period furniture, the
rooms exhibit paintings, scores, and sketches for theatre
sets. Open: Tue-Sun 9.00-12.15 hrs and 13.00-16.30 hrs.
Entrance AS 25. *See map fig. 41.*

Schubert's Birthplace, Nussdorfer Strasse 54
This building where Schubert was born in 1797 comprised a series of tiny two-room apartments. The Schuberts were 14 in family, and Franz was born in the kitchen. Open-air Schubert performances are sometimes given in the courtyard, and there's also a small concert room on the ground floor.
Open: Tue-Sun 9.00-12.15 & 13.00-16.30 hrs. Entrance AS 25.
In District 9, served by trams 37 or 38 from Schottentor.

Haydn's Residence, Haydngasse 19
Among the objects displayed are letters, manuscripts and personal possessions as well as two pianos and the death-mask of the composer.
Open: Tue-Sun 9.00-12.15 & 13.00-16.30 hrs. Entrance AS 25. Located in District 6. Take Subway Line U3; get off at Zieglergasse, ask directions and walk.

Beethoven – House of the Heiligenstadt Testament, Probusgasse 6
In this 3-roomed apartment in Heiligenstadt (19th District), Beethoven composed his Symphony No. 2. Here, in 1802, he became acutely conscious of his deafness. Looking out from his window he could see the bells ringing at the neighbouring church – but he couldn't hear them. That's when he made his last Will and Testament, saying that a deaf composer could have nothing left to live for.

He went on living for another 25 years, composing music but hearing nothing.
Open: Tue-Sun 9.00-12.15 & 13.00-16.30 hrs. Entrance AS 30.
By public transport: U-Bahn U4 or U6 to Heiligenstadt; then about four stops on Bus 38A to Armbrustergasse.

Districts 2 and 3

Vienna's 2nd District is wedged between the Danube Canal and the Danube River. Sightseeing interest focusses mainly on the Prater and the Ferris Wheel (see Nightlife section 2.10). Johann Strauss lived for several years in a first-floor apartment at Praterstrasse 54, where he composed innumerable waltzes including *The Blue Danube*. Downstairs is now a McDonald's, where they compose hamburgers.

At the Danube River, a very long and thin island splits the present-day main channel. Danube Island was inaugurated in 1881 as a big recreation area, and is well equipped with beaches, cycle paths, playgrounds and sport facilities.

Rearing up on the opposite shore is the 817-ft Danube Tower which includes an observation platform, and then a café and a restaurant which revolve at different speeds.

Close by are the huge tower blocks of the Vienna International Center (better known as UNO-City), the home of numerous UN agencies. The adjoining Austria Center Vienna is the city's largest conference hall.

Returning over the Danube Canal it's worth making a detour to see the **Hundertwasser House** in District 3, at Löwengasse and Kegelgasse. This showpiece of municipal housing is a delightful fantasy in colour and architectural design. Don't miss it! Tram N takes you there.

2.6 Take a trip

Much depends on whether you are on a 3-day or a 7-day City Break. During a shorter stay, there's barely time for just one out-of-town excursion. The top choice is a half-day Vienna Woods coach tour, featuring visits to Heiligenkreuz Monastery and Mayerling. During a longer break, it's worth adding a whole-day Danube cruise.

Vienna Woods

For a budget-priced view of the Vienna Woods, go to Heiligenstadt station (U-Bahn U4 or U6 or Tram D), and catch Bus 38A. The route goes through Grinzing wine-village (see Nightlife section 2.10) and thence to the viewpoints of Cobenzl, Kahlenberg and Leopoldsberg.

For walkers there are innumerable footpaths down from these hilltops. From Cobenzl you can walk back to Grinzing through woods which inspired much of Beethoven's *Pastoral Symphony*. It's also possible to cut across to the rival wine village of Sievering, and thence by 39A bus back to Heiligenstadt.

The Mayerling story

Coach tours to Mayerling and Heiligenkreuz take a different route, southwards along idyllic valleys much loved by Franz Schubert and his friends.

The standard tour includes a stop at a disused gypsum mine used for underground aircraft assembly during the last war, and now developed as a tourist attraction with a boat ride on Europe's largest subterranean lake.

Highlight of the trip is the 12th-century Cistercian Monastery of Heiligenkreuz, beautifully located in the heart of the Vienna Woods about 20 miles outside the city. Some 16 monks remain, devoting themselves to monastery upkeep.

Close by is the hunting lodge of Mayerling, where Archduke Rudolf, heir to the throne, committed suicide with his mistress Maria Vetsera in January 1889. Dozens of books have been written about the affair.

The return journey along the Schwechat river valley then passes by Baden, famed since Roman times for its sulphurous hot springs. The extensive vineyards of Gumpoldskirchen produce a popular wine.

Blue Danube?

Go to Vienna, without seeing the Danube? That's quite possible if you just stay entirely in the centre, where the only waterway is the uninspiring Danube Canal.

Most travellers want to make their own decision on that controversial question: What colour is the Danube? In fact, Strauss's favourite river is only blue if seen in the right light and with the right colour spectacles. For much of its distance, the Danube is a luscious treacle of brown mud scooped from the Bavarian plains, mingled with greyish-green from limestone deposits of the River Inn. Near the start of a Danube cruise trip, watch for the huge refuse incinerator which doubles as a tourist attraction thanks to design and decoration of the facade by the Viennese painter Hundertwasser.

The most beautiful part of the Danube near Vienna is called the Wachau, which stretches 20 miles between Dürnstein and Melk. This wine district features romantic scenery. At every river bend are smiling villages set among orchards, with age-old churches, monasteries and castles to complete the scenic perfection. At Dürnstein Richard Lionheart was held to enormous ransom on his way back in 1193 from the 3rd Crusade.

Melk

Most remarkable is Melk Monastery. Built upon a granite rock dominating the river, the Benedictine abbey occupies the site of a Roman encampment. One gallery alone of the magnificent Baroque building is nearly 200 yards long.

Exploration of this area requires at least a full day – whether by rented car, coach-and-steamer tour, or by public transport. Shorter Danube cruises are operated mainly from the landing stage at Schwedenplatz on the Danube Canal, to give an hour on the main stream.

2.7 Sunday in Vienna

Shops are tightly closed on Sundays, and the centre of Vienna can then have a somewhat dead appearance.

So, on Sunday, concentrate on general sightseeing and museums (bearing in mind that most museums are closed on Monday or Tuesday). Ask your tour rep for details of coach excursions that operate on Sundays. Villages of the Vienna Woods are lively with daytime visitors from the city, escaping to the wine-gardens.

For a religious service there is choice of 365 Catholic churches. Consider a short list of the Karlskirche for a service in early 18th-century Baroque surroundings; or St. Stephen's cathedral.

For non-Catholic services, check with the following phone numbers: Anglican 7131575; Lutheran 5128392; Methodist 786367; Jewish 361655; Islamic 301389.

Vienna Boys' Choir

Seats for Sunday Mass sung by the Vienna Boys' Choir at the Imperial Chapel of the Hofburg should be booked at least eight weeks in advance. Write to Hofmusik-kapelle, Hofburg, A-1010 Vienna, Austria. Seats are priced from AS 60 to 310.

Don't enclose cash, but pick up the reserved tickets at the Burgkapelle on the previous Friday between 11-13 hrs or on Sunday between 8.30 and 9.00 hrs. The service itself starts at 9.15 a.m.

Otherwise, try queuing at the Chapel between 15 and 17 hrs on Friday when a limited number of tickets are sold. The only remaining chance without prior booking is to queue on Sunday from 8.30 hrs (or earlier) for standing room which is free.

The services are held every Sunday and religious holiday from mid-September till June. Don't expect to *see* the choir! By tradition the singers are out of sight in the choir loft.

The Boys' Choir can also be heard (and seen!) at 15.30 hrs every Friday in May, June, September and October at the Lichtental Church at Marktgasse 40.

Ticket reservations cost around AS 390 or 430 from Reisebüro Mondial, Faulmanngasse 4, A-1040 Vienna. Tel: (1) 588040 extension 141.

2.8 Shopping

On Monday, with museums closed, you can catch up on shop-gazing. Shop hours are normally Monday to Saturday 9-18 hrs. Vienna is a window-shoppers' paradise, though most of the luxury items seem pricey by UK standards. Shops in the central district offer a turn-of-the-century elegance, with high fashion at high prices.

Most visitors stroll along the Kärntnerstrasse, linking the State Opera House and St. Stephen's Cathedral with shops all the way. Specially delightful is the atmosphere of the Graben, with its outdoor cafés, street entertainers, luxury shops and an elegant clientele. The Graben and the neighbouring Kohlmarkt are Vienna's Bond Street. Vienna's Oxford Street is Mariahilferstrasse, where prices are closer to what average Viennese can afford.

Specially worth admiring is the craftware: glass, hand-painted porcelain, decorative ceramics, bronze, pewter and silver. Other favourite items are petit point, enamel fashion jewelry, wrought-iron work and leather goods.

In this city so preoccupied with the past, many side streets are dotted with stores that deal in antiques, old coins, books and stamps.

Antique furniture and objets d'art from Habsburg times can be found especially around Josefplatz – Augustinerstrasse, Plankengasse, Dorotheergasse and Spiegelgasse.

Auctions

Regular art and antique auctions are held at the state-run
Dorotheum at Dorotheergasse 17, which originally was
founded in 1788 as a Pawn Shop. Today the Dorotheum
ranks among the great auction houses of Europe. Articles
can be inspected Mon-Fri 10-18 hrs, Sat 9-12 hrs.

At the other price extreme is the Naschmarkt flea
market, close to Opern Ring. It's open every Saturday
from 8 a.m. till around 4 or 6 p.m., depending when
stall-holders feel like calling it a day. *See map fig. 28.*

On offer is everything from low-grade textiles to col-
lectors' items like watches and clocks, coins, first-day
covers, books, glassware and pottery. Buyers come from
all over Europe. It's worth an hour or two, especially
when most Saturday afternoons are blank for shoppers.

Naschmarkt is also Vienna's most important and
colourful retail food market, open every day with a great
selection of fruit, vegetables and all other foodstuffs.

2.9 Eating out in Vienna

The coffeehouse scene

The Viennese ritual of coffee-drinking has thrived ever
since 1683, when a retreating Turkish army left behind
sacks of mysterious beans. A Pole called Kolschitzky
knew how many beans make a beverage, and opened the
first coffeehouse. The Viennese did not like the bitter
taste of the Turkish drink, so Kolschitzky added cream
and sugar. He prospered. Soon the custom of drinking
Viennese-style coffee had spread throughout Europe.

The Viennese pride themselves as coffee connoisseurs.
They would never dream of merely ordering 'a cup of
coffee'. The exact ingredients and their proportions must
be specified – coffee, milk, cream, whipped cream –
each permutation having its technical name.

For most visitors, the favourite is Melange – half-
milk, half-coffee, with an optional dollop of whipped
cream. Most other coffees are very strong, such as Brauner, Mokka and Espresso. These can be either grosse or
kleine – large or small. The coffee is served with a glass
of water, to help clear the palate.

Part of the Vienna life-style is to have coffee and cake
in the afternoon. Every Viennese has his own preferred
coffee house and is very fussy about it. The more elegant
establishments are a sedate and leisured bolt-hole to escape the 20th century. Several coffeehouses are very
famous and expensive, but there is also wide choice of
cafés at more modest prices.

Among the most renowned is **Sacher's**, just behind the
State Opera House. The establishment is world famed for
its rich and moist dark chocolate cake – the Sachertorte,
a great Viennese speciality. For Melange and Sachertorte,
both piled with whipped cream, you can expect a £5 bill.

Coffee with elegance

In the very up-market street called Kohlmarkt (which means Coal Market) is **Demel's** at no. 14, which is the most old-fashioned coffeehouse in Vienna. Like Sacher's, it is expensive but the atmosphere is delightful. Forget your waistline and sample the beautiful cakes, pastries and savoury snacks served with 19th-century formality. They also sell individually made and boxed chocolates.

Sirk, small and elegant at 53 Kärntnerstrasse, was a former supplier to the court. Less expensive is **Heiner's**, with two branches – at 21 Kärntner Strasse and at 9 Wollzeile – with excellent cakes and pastries, and very good coffee.

Café Mozart on Albertinaplatz also offers elegance and tradition.

For more exploration of Vienna's café scene, here's a short-list of recommendations – all in 1st District, or very close. They also serve other beverages, and often can provide snacks or light meals from a limited menu.

Large and moderately priced

Café Schwarzenberg, on the Ring facing Schwarzenbergerplatz. Menu available. Piano music in the evening.
Café Landtmann, on the Ring opposite City Hall. Large terrace. Famous for its choice of 32 different types of coffee. Menu available.
Café Tyrol, on Albertina Platz. Art deco interior, quiet and pleasant. Small snacks available.
Café Central, on Herrengasse in 1st district. Traditional, frequented by locals. This was the haunt of Vienna's turn-of-the-century intelligentsia. Menu available.
Café Raimund opposite the Volkstheater. Pleasant, spacious, reasonable prices, and a menu is available.
Café Melange on Lichtensteg, beyond St. Stephens on the left. Very pleasant, and quite traditional.
Café Sluka, right beside the City Hall. Very pleasant, and menu available.
Café Museum on Karlsplatz, opposite Secession. Arty, in art deco style.

Small, out-of-the-way and trendy

Kleines Café, on Franziskanerplatz is small and quiet, except at night. Reasonable prices. No menu, only cakes.
Café Hawelka on Dorotheergasse, just off the Graben. Frequented by academics, artists, writers and students of music and literature. Always full!   Closed on Tuesdays. Looks dark and dingy, but full of character and local Bohemian atmosphere. Reasonable prices.
Café Corso, Neuer Markt. Small and friendly, with terrace. Snacks and cakes, reasonable prices.
Café Eiles on the corner of Josefstädter Strasse, near City Hall. Menu available.

Fast coffee

Whenever you need refreshment in Vienna, there's always plentiful choice, especially within the Ring. Many coffeehouses are called Café Konditorei, where you can buy chocolates as well as drinks and pastries. Lowest cost are the stand-up coffee-bars where you can have a Mocca or a Brauner – small for 50p, big for £1 – or a Melange for 75p. For comparison, these bars also sell an Achtel (one-eighth litre) of wine, white or red, for 50p.

There are several chains of cafés such as **Aida** and **Janele** where prices are reasonable. Another institution is the **EduScho** coffee chain, which sells coffee beans and ground coffee, claimed to be the best in Austria. As a taster, they offer a small Espresso for 40p, or double size for 80p. EduScho is not a place to relax – stand-up drinking only – but it's great if you just want a strong coffee to pep you up.

The lunch scene

A traditional Viennese meal usually consists of soup, meat dish and a sweet. The main meal is normally at midday, but most visitors prefer something light at noon, saving themselves for an evening splurge.

For a quick lunch, watch for the chalked-up day's menu on blackboards outside cafés and restaurants – usually soup and main course for around £4 or £5. If you go à la carte, most main dishes in average restaurants cost about £5. Many park cafés feature reasonably-priced snacks. At hot-dog stands, a pair of Frankfurters with bread and mustard could cost £1.60. If sunny weather tempts you to a park picnic, you can get supplies from supermarkets. There are two, opposite the State Opera House. At a delicatessen, all kinds of cheese and cold meats are priced Austrian style in units of *dag*, which stands for Dekagramm. 10 dag = 100 grammes, or about a quarter pound. Purchases will be neatly parcelled, ready for a picnic at any of the delightful parks around the Ring. Very pleasant and central is the Burggarten.

The restaurant scene

Vienna offers bewildering restaurant choice of every type and grade. The most traditional eating places are the 'Keller' and the 'Beisl' – cellars and inns. A 'Kloster-keller' – monastery cellar – offers a wider range of wines. There are also 'Heurigen-Restaurants' which are traditional wine taverns found mainly in wine-growing suburbs outside the city – at Grinzing, for example. However, a few are located in the city centre, and call themselves 'Stadtheuriger'. They are always very friendly with lots of character, atmosphere and local colour. Vienna also has a wide range of more formal restaurants – luxury, intimate or foreign-cuisine. Some restaurants close during July-August for a month or more.

City-centre eating

If you just want to wander round, dropping in somewhere that takes your fancy, there are three central areas of inexpensive bars and restaurants that stand shoulder to shoulder.

Away from the higher-cost establishments of the Kärntner Strasse and Graben district, explore the little area behind St. Stephen's Cathedral: along Sonnenfels-gasse, Schönlaterngasse, and part of Bäckerstrasse. It's a very old part of the city, where good-value restaurants, cafés and wine-bars offer tradition and local colour.

Typical is **Figlmüller**'s, who specialise in giant Wiener Schnitzels. It's a small restaurant located in a narrow alley between two parallel streets, Wollzeile and Bäckerstrasse. There's no printed menu: just a blackboard with prices. Figlmuller closes at 15 hrs on Saturdays, and stays closed on Sundays and public holidays. Best to book. Tel: 5126177. *See map, near fig. 41.*

Another little area – quite close – is located around St. Rupert's Church, the oldest in the city, to the left of Rotenturm Strasse. Locals call the district The Bermuda Triangle (Bermudadreieck). It's a network of cobbled streets, lined with cafés, trendy restaurants, Beisls and bars, and is particularly lively by night.

The Spittelberg area, in District 7 behind the Art History Museum is an historic conservation area that is well worth finding. From the Volkstheater, go up Burg-gasse. Three parallel streets comprise this corner of old Vienna: Gutenberg-Gasse, Spittelberg-Gasse and Schrank-Gasse. Along the cobbled streets, lined with historic houses, is a delightful mixture of Austrian, French and Italian-style restaurants and street cafés. On summer evenings the area has a lively atmosphere, thanks partly to a small local theatre.

For something unusual and intimate, though a bit more expensive, try the very small, old-fashioned Biedermeier restaurant called **Zum ebene Erde zum erster Stock** at Burggasse 13. At ground level and first floor, it's rated among the best restaurants of Vienna.

Restaurant Guide

Following is a short selection of restaurants in the different categories – mostly in the middle price-range of £10 to £20 for a meal.

Keller-restaurants

Augustinerkeller, on Augustinerstrasse facing Albertina Platz. In 'town Heuriger' style, on two floors with live music – violin, accordian, guitar. Excellent food and good value. *See map between figs. 1 and 29.*

Rathauskeller, located in the Town Hall itself. Choice of restaurants, some with music. Elegant and traditional with excellent food and good value. *See map fig. 12.*

Piaristenkeller, at Piaristengasse 45 in the 8th district. The best of its type in Vienna, in an old cloister. Zither music, extensive menu, good value.

Esterhazykeller, at Haarhof 1, just off Naglergasse in the 1st district. Cosy, out-of-the-way, with terrace, good food and reasonable prices. *See map, near fig. 35.*

Urbanikeller, on Am Hof, one of the most impressive squares in Vienna. It ranks among the oldest and best Kellers in the city, with traditional cuisine, Austrian wine and music. *See map fig. 35.*

Lindenkeller, at Rotenturmstrasse 12. Vienna's oldest restaurant, dated 1435. Terrace, very traditional, no music. *See map, near fig. 39.*

Zwölf Apostelkeller, at Sonnenfelsgasse 3. Historic surroundings in underground gothic cloister. Mainly a wine cellar with snacks such as soup and sausages. No music, apart from the clock. *See map, between figs. 39 & 15.*

'Beisl'

Griechenbeisl, Fleischmarkt 11, next to the Greek Orthodox church (along Rotenturm Strasse from *fig. 38*, then right). This is the oldest restaurant in Vienna. It has several rooms, but everyone wants to dine where walls and ceiling are covered by reproduction signatures of famous guests like Mozart and Beethoven. Excellent food and service, with fabulous atmosphere and zither music.

A reservation is very necessary. Non-reserved clients can be fitted into the Augustiner rooms, a more recent extension upstairs, with much less atmosphere.

Stadtbeisl, Naglergasse 21 in 1st district, with a summer terrace. Quiet and cosy, with good food and reasonable prices. Lovely atmosphere. *See map, near fig. 35.*

S'Müllerbeisl, Seilerstätte 15. Small, with a cellar restaurant. Good food, value and service. No music.

Glacisbeisl, Messepalast, situated in the Museum quarter. Inexpensive, very traditional, with all sorts of speciality dishes including vegetarian cuisine.

Vegetarian

Siddhartha, Fleischmarkt 16, 1st District.

Wrenkh, Hollergasse 9, 15th District; and at Bauernmarkt 10, 1st District.

Other restaurants

Smutny, on Elizabethstrasse. Full of local colour and ambiance, with very simple decor. Noted for its lengthy menu, excellent draught beer and reasonable prices. Surroundings and waiters seem untouched by time!

Gigerl, opposite the British Bookshop on Ballgasse. Small, Heuriger-style, but quite expensive. Good food.

Ofenloch, Kurrentgasse 8, just off the Judenplatz. Very popular, cosy turn-of-the-century atmosphere. Good food, quite expensive.

Paulusstube, Walfischgasse 7 near State Opera, with garden terrace. Very old and cosy, music, good food, reasonable prices, but slow service.

Carrousel Vienne, Krugerstrasse 1. Quite large, not traditional, but very reasonable prices.

Chains of restaurants

Wienerwald restaurants specialise in modest-priced chicken dishes. Very good value, good food and service.

Naschmarkt – large restaurants with varied menu. Specially good value is the menu of the day.

Nordsee – self-service fish restaurants. Excellent fish, reasonable prices. Also take-away snacks.

2.10 Nightlife

Like all European capitals, Vienna has the usual quota of nightlife, from clip-joint strip clubs to sophisticated international cabaret shows and high-rolling Casinos.

Vienna's cultural life reaches its peak during winter months, with theatre and concert performances virtually every night. The Carnival Season, called Fasching, brings high-spirited festivities to January and February.

For music in more popular style, the village suburbs on the edge of the Vienna Woods feature wine taverns where traditional Viennese folk music is played year-round. The custom is to drink new wine - called *Heuriger* - and never mind next morning's hangover!

Sign of the Bush

Traditionally, when the new wine has fermented out, mine host invites custom by hanging a pine-tree branch on a pole outside his door. That is the "Sign of the Bush", a symbol since Roman days of a wine-tavern. Mostly these taverns are family operated, and theoretically they sell only wine from their own vineyards. In practice that is no longer so, but the tradition remains.

The taverns have a centuries'-old charm of their own. Well-scrubbed benches and tables are built solidly of two-inch planks that barely quiver at the most boisterous treatment. On summer evenings, customers sit out in lantern-lit gardens. When nights turn chilly, they migrate into the lime-washed parlours.

Drinking rough new wine is an acquired taste. But you can always order 'old' wine – that is, of the previous year's vintage – for a little extra cost. There are no wine lists. Vintages and years are for the connoisseurs, who frequent the 'monastery cellars' and wine parlours of the inner city. You drink either new or old, red or white, served in quarter-litre tumblers, straight from the barrel. After your throat has got used to the rough edge, life can become very rosy. That's when even the most solemn characters link arms, sing, and buy comic hats.

Wine and song

In the *Heuriger* taverns you hear the authentic folk-songs of Vienna: sentimental or comic, according to the singer's mood. Even to a German linguist, the words are difficult to follow, being sung in the thick Viennese dialect that is baffling as London's cockney to the foreigner.

"Schrammel-music tonight" the larger tavern-owners proclaim. A Schrammel quartet – named after the Brothers Schrammel who popularized this form of music in 19th-century Vienna – consists usually of an accordion player, guitarist, violinist and a singer. The repertoire is traditional. Other taverns feature a zither-player and an accordionist.

Food is available usually in hot and cold buffet style. Just go to the self-service counter, pick what you want, and pay on the spot.

These taverns are concentrated especially in the villages of **Grinzing**, **Sievering**, **Nussdorf** and **Heiligenstadt**, in the northwest suburbs that merge into the Vienna Woods. They are easily accessible from central Vienna by tram or bus.

Go round the Ring to Schottentor. Then take Tram 38 which goes direct to Grinzing, the last stop, in 25 minutes.

Wander into any of the taverns on the main street, and stay wherever takes your fancy. Bear in mind that the transport system closes down at midnight. The last tram from Grinzing runs at 11.50. Avoid an expensive taxi journey!

The Prater

Still on the popular level, another centre of Vienna's night-life is the Prater. Originally a royal game preserve, the vast park was opened to the public in 1766. Stretching to the banks of the Danube, the park is a favourite daytime promenade. By night, everything focusses upon the Wurstelprater – the Fun Fair.

Best evenings for a visit are Saturdays and Sundays. On other nights, the Prater languishes.

Dominating the amusement park is the Big Wheel – the Riesenrad. It was designed by British engineers, prefabricated in England, and erected in Vienna in 1901. There is nothing wildly thrilling about riding on the Ferris Wheel, despite its melodramatic star role in *The Third Man* film.

Movement is barely perceptible, with frequent stops to load new passengers into the cabins. A complete ride can take about 20 minutes, giving ample time to enjoy a magnificent view over Vienna, while poised 220 feet above ground level. Cost is AS 50.

Below are the usual fairground attractions, and restaurant gardens that do brisk trade in beer, sausages and wine.

Opera and Ballet

For any devotee of classical music, a visit to the State
Opera House is one of life's great experiences. The Viennese love of opera is contagious. Even those who normally scorn opera can fall under the spell of this national
institution. Tickets for ever-popular favourites like
"Magic Flute", "Don Giovanni," "Tosca" or "Madame
Butterfly" are usually instantly sold out. But there's always a chance! For less popular works, tickets are
much easier. An alternative, not so 'glamorous', is to
console yourself with the Volksoper, which specialises
mainly in light opera and the big favourites.

Tickets are available at booking agencies around town
which charge an officially approved 25% mark-up. If a
hotel concierge obtains 'impossible' tickets through some
mysterious source, the mark-up can even reach 60%.

Buying tickets direct

Clued-up travellers dodge the mark-ups by going direct to
the central booking office behind the State Opera House,
by Albertina Platz. On the city tourist map, it's marked
by a black triangle. A sign *Bundestheaterkassen* points
the entrance into a courtyard, to the large and efficient
booking hall, highly computerized.

An indicator board shows whether seats are still on
general sale, or sold out. Often, some seats are left with
a restricted view – for instance in the second or third
rows of boxes; or high up, at the side. Even if you have
a terrible seat, the experience is still worth having.
There's nothing to stop you hearing the music in all its
full glory!

The booking office is open Monday to Friday from 8
till 18 hrs; Saturdays 9-14 hrs; Sundays and public holidays from 9-12 hrs. You cannot advance-buy tickets
earlier than seven days before the performance. Staatsoper prices go from a maximum of 2300 Schillings down
to about 100 AS for seats with minimal view. The Volksoper price range is from 650 or 850 AS downwards. If
you're continuing to Budapest, you can even buy tickets
for the Budapest Opera.

In the expensive State Opera seats, you'll be surrounded by elegance. Even in the gallery there are black
ties and dinner suits among the audience. Standing is
available but only by long queuing before the performance.

For **classical concerts**, there is bewildering variety
year-round: in the Musikverein (home of the Vienna
Philharmonic Orchestra) and the Konzerthaus (Vienna
Symphonic), in the arcaded courtyard of City Hall, in the
splendid Palais Auersperg or in the Church of the Augus-
tinian Friars. Ask your hotel desk or tour rep for the
detailed monthly programme published by the Vienna
Tourist Board.

Night Tours

Travel agencies offer several choices of conducted 'Vienna by Night' circuits. Normally they include several aspects of Vienna: a general tour of the illuminations including the Ring and the Prater, a drink in a traditional coffee house with suitable background music, and possibly Grinzing for Heuriger wine and music.

On Wednesday nights it's possible to include an evening performance of the Lippizaner horses at the Spanish Riding School. The more expensive jaunts include a night club show.

2.11 At your service

Banks and Exchange Bureaux

General opening hours for banks are Monday-Friday 08.00-12.30 and 13.30-15.00 hours (17.30 hrs on Thursday). Travel Agencies exchange money during business hours Mon-Sat. An exchange bureau is open daily except Sundays in the Opernpassage (the underpass by the State Opera House). Exchange bureaux are open till 22 hrs at Westbahnhof (West Station) and Südbahnhof (South Station); at the Airport until 23 hrs.

On arrival, avoid the exchange bureau in the airport baggage hall which gives lower-than-average pay-out. The best deals are at main Post Offices which conduct exchange business, charging nil commission. In contrast, exchange bureaux charge a minimum commission which can be disproportionate on small transactions. In central areas, bank machines can recognise and exchange most Western currencies, and give reasonable rates even on relatively small-value banknotes. Very handy!

Post Office and Telephone

Opening hours: Weekdays 8-12 & 14-18 hrs.
General Post Office: 9 Fleischmarkt 1
Main railway station post offices are open weekends and late at night. Stamps are also sold at tobacconists, souvenir shops and from vending machines in front of most post offices.

International Phone Calls

Check the cost of long distance calls from your hotel before phoning as these may be very expensive. Save money on international calls by phoning from a Post Office or from a call box. For local city calls, insert one Schilling coin and dial the number.

To call UK, insert at least AS 14 which gives you one minute. Follow the dialling instructions in section 1.3 of this book. If you're making several long-distance calls, consider buying a phonecard or "Wertkarte" at post offices. Cost: AS 50 for the lowest-price card.

Emergency Phone Numbers

Police	133
Fire Brigade	122
Ambulance	144
Red Cross	5546460

Emergency Medical Service

Daytime	531153
Night	5500

Other useful Phone Numbers and Addresses

British Consulate, 3 Jauresgasse 10	7146117
U.S. Consulate, Gartenbaupromenade 10	31339
Canadian Consulate, Schubertring 12	5333691
Australian Consulate, 4 Mattiellistrasse 2-4	5128580

Vienna Tourist Information, Kärntnerstrasse 38, daily 9-19 hrs.
The Vienna Tourist Board produces free maps and listings for hotels, restaurants, museums, and the monthly What's On. They also publish an excellent sightseeing guide "Vienna from A to Z", price AS 30.

Austrian National Tourist Office, Margaretenstrasse 1 (corner of Wiedner Hauptstrasse in the 4th district) – for information about other regions of Austria.
Open: Mon-Fri 9-17 hrs.   Tel: 431 60 813

Chemists (Apotheke)

For night and Sunday service, all chemists display the address of the nearest Apotheke on duty. Otherwise, try International Apotheke, 17 Kärntner-Ring 1. Tel: 1550. Open: Mon-Fri 8-12 & 14-18 hrs; Sat 8-12 hrs.

Lost Property

If you lose something, contact the nearest police station. After three days try Vienna's main Lost and Found office at 9 Wasagasse 22. Tel: 313440. Open: Mon-Fri 8-13 hrs. The nearest U-Bahn is Schottentor (U2).

Chapter Three

Salzburg

3.1 Introduction

Music and enchanting city sightseeing combine to make Salzburg an ideal City Break destination. A huge bonus is that Salzburg is gateway to Austria's most scenic region – the Salzkammergut of idyllic lakes and mountains.

The musical scene operates year-round, to include Carnival (Fasching) with masked balls from early January until Shrove Tuesday, an annual Mozart Week in late January, an Easter Festival, Whitsun Concerts, the world-famous Summer Festival, and so through the year till Christmas. December is marked by numerous Christmas exhibitions and cribs, a Christmas Market in the Cathedral Square, decorations and carols everywhere.

Salzburg offers constant reminders that Mozart was born here in 1756. Many chamber performances are given in historical rooms where the young prodigy first astonished his audiences more than two centuries ago.

The Salzburg Festival, running from late July and throughout August, is the highlight of the annual calendar. World radio and TV focusses on the major operas and orchestral concerts and the morality play *Everyman*, performed in front of the cathedral. But there are over a hundred other Festival performances, including serenade concerts by candlelight, chamber music in the Mozarteum, organ recitals in the cathedral, Sunday mass with orchestra and choir at the Franziskanerkirche.

Frankly, if the musical scene is not your prime interest, it's better to go earlier or later to Salzburg, when the city is less tightly jammed.

Any time of the year, there are photogenic scenes almost anywhere you point a camera: within the age-old city streets, along well-tended paths beside the river or on the hills, all within a few minutes of the centre. Take a bus or a coach tour, and glorious mountain scenery awaits, every season with a different face.

In a two-centre arrangement with Vienna, Salzburg and its mountain setting make a relaxing contrast to the urban delights of the capital. Even the journey between the two cities is a visual pleasure, every mile of the way.

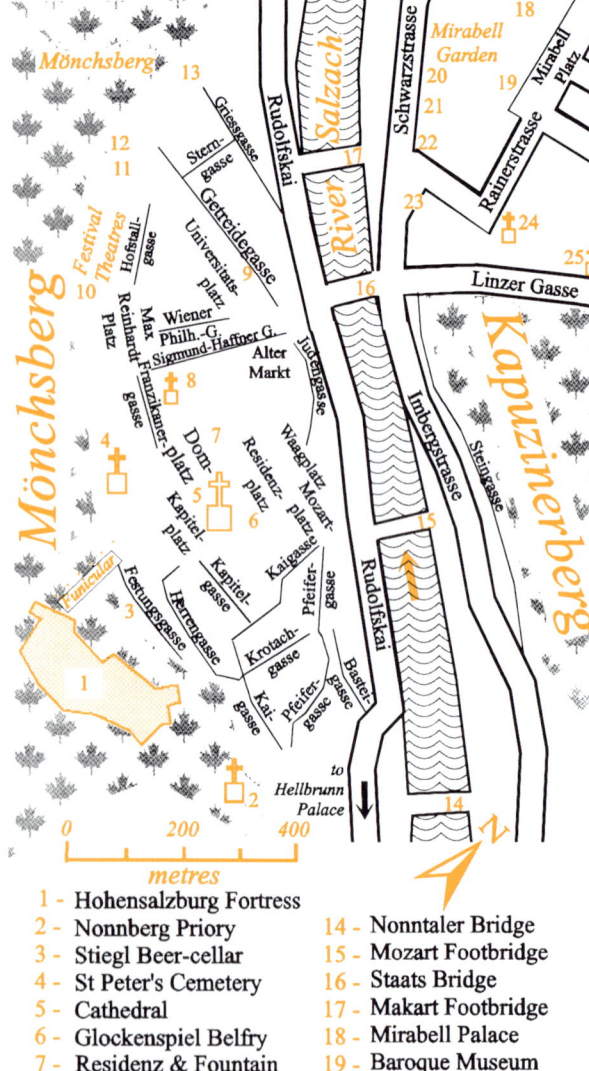

1 - Hohensalzburg Fortress
2 - Nonnberg Priory
3 - Stiegl Beer-cellar
4 - St Peter's Cemetery
5 - Cathedral
6 - Glockenspiel Belfry
7 - Residenz & Fountain
8 - Franciscan Church
9 - Mozart's birthplace
10 - Festival Theatres
11 - Horsepond
12 - Toy Museum
13 - Lift to Mönchsberg

14 - Nonntaler Bridge
15 - Mozart Footbridge
16 - Staats Bridge
17 - Makart Footbridge
18 - Mirabell Palace
19 - Baroque Museum
20 - Mozarteum
21 - Marionette Theatre
22 - Provincial Theatre
23 - Mozart Residence
24 - Holy Trinity Church
25 - St Sebastian's Church

SALZBURG - City Centre

3.2 Arrival in Salzburg

If you're arriving direct to Salzburg airport – 4 kms from Salsburg centre – Bus no. 77 goes to the main railway station. The service runs every 15 minutes Monday to Friday and every 30 minutes Saturday and Sunday. Journey time: 20 minutes. Cost: 22 Schillings.

By taxi, the cost to central hotels from the airport is AS 150 for the journey lasting 15 to 20 minutes. AS 10 extra is payable for each item of luggage in the boot.

Your tour rep or the hotel may be able to arrange a more economical mini-bus transfer for the return journey.

3.3 Public transport

Salzburg is a relatively small city, most hotels are central, and sightseeing highlights are all within easy walking distance. Many visitors make little use of public transport, except for rides on the Fortress funicular or on the Mönchsberg Lift to the Café Winkler terrace.

However, the bus service in Salzburg is frequent, quick, and easy to use. A 24-hour or 72-hour Rover Ticket is good value for anyone making more active use of the local transport network. These tickets are also valid for the funicular, the Mönchsberg Lift and on the urban railway – Lokalbahn – as far as Bergheim.

Taxis

Taxis are expensive, considering the short distances within Salzburg, and are often hard to find. If you do need a taxi it's wise to pre-book:
Salburger Radiotaxi Service (Funktaxi-Vereinigung), Rainerstrasse 27 Tel: 76111 or 77111
Advance bookings Tel: 74400

Bicycle Hire

Many visitors rent a bike for the day, riding along riverside paths. In summer, with good weather, people go to open-air swimming pools. There's one about 10 minutes from the centre, direction Leopoldskron. Or you can cycle to the Gaisberg, which has pretty scenery. Cost of bike-hire is about AS 120 to 150 per day. Take your passport, needed as security deposit. Two addresses:
Main Railway Station, desk 3 Apr-Nov Tel: 71541-337
Tourist Information Office on Mozartplatz.

Horse-cabs

The cab-rank for tourist circuits is in Residenzplatz. *See map fig. 6.* The carriages hold four passengers. For a circuit of about 20-25 minutes, reckon AS 380; for 50 minutes, AS 740.

3.4 Basic Salzburg

If you go overboard on chamber music, Salzburg can keep you happy every evening, year-round. On a short visit, here's a check-list on what else to do.

(1) Wander very slowly along Getreidegasse, shop-gazing, taking pictures of wrought-iron shop signs and peeking into side alleys and courtyards. *See map fig. 9.*

(2) Visit Mozart's birthplace at No. 9 Getreidegasse.

(3) Take the lift (*map fig. 13*) to Café Winkler, admire the view; then walk through hilltop Mönchsberg woodlands to the Festung and down by funicular.

(4) At 11 a.m. or 6 p.m. listen to the Carillon on Residenz Platz. *See map fig. 6.*

(5) At the Marionette Theatre, see puppets performing to opera music recorded from the Salzburg Festival.

(6) Get drenched by the trick fountains of Hellbrunn.

(7) Conjure up memories of *White Horse Inn* or *Sound of Music* by taking an afternoon coach tour of the Salzkammergut lakes.

(8) Try the local soufflé speciality, vanilla-flavoured Salzburger Nockerl.

(9) Admire the flower displays in Mirabell Garden.

(10) Cross the border to Berchtesgaden, and see where Hitler built his "Eagle's Nest".

Orientation

Almost at the centre of Austria, Salzburg is capital of Salzburg province on the northern slopes of the Alps. The medieval riches of the region derived from a salt-mining monopoly – hence the word *Salz* which occurs in the city's name and in the River Salzach which flows through the heart of Salzburg.

Its natural setting is superb. The Romans developed the site as an administrative centre, with one of their main military roads bridging the Salzach.

Building a northern Rome

Later, the prince archbishops of Salzburg established mighty power in the land, building a cathedral overlooked by a massive fortress. Other public buildings clustered at the foot of the Mönchsberg – the "Monks' Mountain" – in the narrow strip of land between the cliff and the river. That's the heart of old Salzburg.

A big name in Salzburg was Wolf Dietrich who became Archbishop in 1587, at age 28. His dream was to make Salzburg the Rome of the North. He laid the initial plans for a rebuilt cathedral modelled on St. Peter's, with an adjoining palace on Residenz Square. His splendid Court Stables are now part of the Salzburg Festival complex. Wolf Dietrich and his 17th-century successors changed the face of Salzburg.

Across the river, another steep hill called the Kapuzin-erberg dominates the newer side of Salzburg, revolving especially around the early 17th-century Schloss Mirabell and its Garden.

All the sites, each side of the river, are within easy walking distance. The standard city sightseeing tours – normally starting from Mirabell Square – show you the basic locations, including a trip out to Hellbrunn Palace.

Buildings and Monuments

NOTE: Entry times and prices are for guidance, and may change. Most entrances are reduced for children, students and senior citizens. Some combined tickets are available. Best Buy is the Salzburg Card, giving you unlimited transport and free entry to 23 key attractions.

Hohensalzburg Fortress

Built over the centuries on an ancient Celtic and Roman site, this is now the largest fully preserved medieval castle in Europe. The present castle dates from 1077, with major enlargements around 1500 completed in 1681.

Take the funicular up to the castle, which offers su-perb views over the city. You can just wander round the fortifications for admission fee of AS 35 or visit the Fortress Museum with a guide for an extra AS 35.

Conducted tours can include a Sound and Vision Show, the Fortress Museum and the Rainer Museum, with displays of weaponry and instruments of torture, mainly from 13th to 15th century. *See map fig. 1.*

Nonnberg Benedictine Convent

Close to the Fortress is the Convent founded 696 AD, when St. Rupert revived a monastic community which led to the medieval expansion of Salzburg. *See map fig. 2.*

See the late-Gothic basilica with crypt, 12th-century frescoes, and St John's Chapel with altar dated 1498.

Cathedral

Located directly below the Fortress, on Domplatz, the Cathedral is the finest early Baroque building north of the Alps and the third to stand on the site. *See map fig. 5.*

The original building founded 778 by St. Virgil (who was an Irish bishop named O'Farrell) was replaced by a late Romanesque edifice which in turn was destroyed by fire in 1598. Today's cathedral was completed in 1628.

The dome was destroyed during World War II but was restored by 1949. The cathedral has a magnificent marble facade, three massive bronze doors (modern, depicting Faith, Hope and Love), a Baroque organ and a Gothic font from 1321.

Organ recitals are usually given Wed and Sat 11.15 a.m. The Festival performance of "Everyman" – life and death of the rich man – is staged on Cathedral Square.

A Cathedral Museum is open May to October 10-17 hrs. Entrance AS 12. The Cathedral excavations can be visited May-Oct 9-17 hrs. Entrance AS 20.

Residenz-Platz

Behind the Cathedral leads into Residentz-Platz, distinguished by the largest (40 feet high) baroque fountain outside of Italy, dated 1661. Along one side of the square, adjoining the Cathedral, is the huge **Residenz** – town house of the Prince Bishops – founded 1120, rebuilt 1619, and now used mainly for expositions and classical concerts. *See map fig. 7.*

The State Rooms are open daily, admission AS 50, with 50-minute conducted tours mostly every half hour from 10 till 16.30 hrs in July and August; at hourly intervals the rest of the year.

The **Residenz Gallery** features 200 paintings of 16th to 19th centuries – Dutch, French, Italian, and Austrian Baroque. Open 10-17 hrs. Admission AS 50. A combined ticket for State Rooms and Gallery costs AS 80.

Opposite on the square is the **Glockenspiel Tower** *(map fig. 6)* rising above the **Residenz New Building**, dating from 1602, which now houses the Central Post Office and the Provincial government. The 35-bell carillon plays tunes by Haydn, Weber and Mozart at 7, 11 and 18 hrs. The chimes are best heard in Residenz Platz.

Mozart Square

Residenz Platz leads into Mozart Square, a lively tourist location containing a central statue of Mozart, erected in 1842. The very clued-up Salzburg Information Office is next door to American Express.

The Shopping Streets

All this area is pedestrianized, and window-shoppers can enjoy walking back beside the Residenz, through the beautiful Alte Markt (Old Market Square) and along Judengasse (formerly part of a ghetto) to Getreidegasse. That richly picturesque cobbled street is famous for dozens of wrought-iron shop signs – many painted or gilded – which hang over the narrow street, giving myriad chances of good photos. In summer, the best time for pictures is around 5 p.m., when afternoon sunshine lights up both sides of the street. Otherwise, Getreidegasse is in shadow most of the day. *See map fig. 9.*

Mozart Museum

Look out for the sausage shop at No. 9 Getreidegasse. Above is Mozart's birthplace, cherished as a museum. The rooms contain a fascinating collection relating to the composer, including his clavichord and first violin, and models of early stage sets from several Mozart operas. Open 9-18 hrs; or till 19 hrs Jul-Aug. Admission AS 70.

Café Winkler

The far end of Getreidegasse leads towards the Mönchs-berg lift *(map fig. 13)* at Gstättengasse 13 – the energy-saving route to the Café Winkler terrace which offers the finest overall view of Salzburg.

Horse-pond and Festival Theatres

On Sigmundsplatz is the astonishing trough built in 1695 for the Prince-Archbishops' 130 horses. Lively frescoes and statues in this monumental construction mask a for-mer quarry. *See map fig. 11.*

Next door *(fig. 10)* was the court riding school and stable, which now form part of the Festspielhaus complex where major works are performed during the annual Festival. Outside the July-August period, one or two conducted tours are made of the Festival Halls and Thea-tre, daily except Sun, at either 11 or 15 hrs. Fee: AS 30.

Franciscan Church

Past the Festspielhaus and towards the Cathedral is the Franziskanerkirche, founded 1221 with a Romanesque nave, 15th-century Gothic choir, 17th-century side cha-pels and a baroque High Altar from 1711. *Map fig. 8.*

St. Peter's Churchyard

Next comes the Monastery of St. Peter – the oldest sur-viving monastery in German-speaking lands, founded late 7th century but with a community established even in mid-5th century. Backing onto the sheer rock face of the Mönchsberg is a remarkable cemetery *(fig. 4),* packed with tombs of leading Salzburg families. Catacombs can be visited, with 20-minute tours at hourly intervals.

Mozart's Residence, Makartplatz 8

Cross the river on the footbridge called Makartsteg *(see map fig. 17)*, which leads direct to Markartplatz where the Mozart family lived from 1773 to 1787 while he wrote over 150 works. *See map fig. 23.* Owing to war damage, all that remains of the original building are the entrance and the "Tanzmeister Saal" which is now a museum devoted to Mozart's life and work during the years 1773-1780. Open 10-18 hrs. Entry AS 65.

Filling the end of the square is the Church of the Holy Trinity *(fig. 24)* a masterpiece built in 1699 by the Vien-nese architect Fischer von Erlach, the genius of Austrian baroque. Frescoes are by Michael Rottmayr, who also worked with Erlach on St. Charles' Church in Vienna.

Mozarteum

To complete the Mozart pilgrimage, go back to the Pro-vincial Theatre *(fig. 22.)* on the corner of Schwarzstrasse. Next door is the Marionette Theatre *(fig. 21.)*, which includes five Mozart operas in its puppet repertoire. The Salzburg Card gives reduced-price admission to a unique performance. Don't miss this experience!

Then comes the Mozarteum *(fig. 20.)*, an Academy of Music – home of the International Mozarteum Foundation – which also operates summer courses. Occasional orchestral concerts are held in the main hall, which rates among the world's finest. In the bastion garden behind the Mozarteum is set a little summer-house originally from Vienna, where Mozart composed *The Magic Flute* in 1791. Visits only during July-August.

Schloss Mirabell and Garden

Next to Makartplatz is the garden of Mirabell Palace, built around 1610 by Archbishop Wolf Dietrich for his Jewish mistress and their twelve children. *See map fig. 18.* The grounds and Greek-mythology statues were later designed by Fischer von Erlach, to include an open-air theatre and a Bastion Garden which afterwards was populated with stone dwarfs. During the height of summer, young people dibble their feet in the Pegasus fountain. A superb view looks across to Salzburg Castle.

Much rebuilt, the palace is now the Mayor's official residence, while the Marble Room is used for concerts and weddings. The ceremonial Angel Staircase is decorated not with angels but cupids.

Within the complex is a Baroque Museum, open Tue-Sat 9-12 and 14-17 hrs; Sun 9-12 hrs. Entrance AS 40. *See map fig. 19.* Outside, on Mirabell Platz, is departure point for sightseeing tours.

Hellbrunn Palace

From Mirabell Platz bus no. 55 goes direct to Hellbrunn Palace – across the river, along Rudolfskai and thence along Alpenstrasse. This early baroque country retreat was built 1612-1615 for Markus Sittikus, who succeeded his uncle Wolf Dietrich as Prince-Archbishop.

Markus Sittikus had somewhat worldly pleasures for a bishop. Judging by the statuary, his favourite god was Bacchus. His fun came from drenching elegant guests with trick fountains, which still operate very effectively.

Also worth seeing are the Stone Theatre where the first Italian operas were performed north of the Alps, and the one-month castle – built in record time, and now housing the Salzburg Folklore Museum (entry AS 20).

Open Easter to October, 9-17 hrs. Entrance is free to the Park, Orangery and Pheasant Reserve. Conducted tours of the Palace and Trick Fountains cost AS 90.

In July and August there are additional evening tours from 18 to 22 hrs - but not during special events.

Remember that the Salzburg Card gives free entry to all the above sites and to those listed in the next section. The card costs AS 200 for 24 hours; AS 270 for 48 hours; AS 360 for 72 hours; and is valid for transport.

3.5 Other sights in Salzburg

St Sebastian's Cemetery, Linzergasse 43

Commissioned by Wolf Dietrich in the manner of an Italian "campo santo", it contains the Prince Archbishop's mausoleum – a magnificent tiled chapel dedicated to Archangel Gabriel. Here also are tombs of the Mozart and Weber families, including Mozart's father Leopold, Mozart's wife Constanze, and her second husband Nikolaus von Nissen. *See map fig. 25.*

Kapuzinerberg

To reach one of Salsburg's best viewpoints, start from Linzergasse, through the archway at No. 14. It's a very steep climb past carved Stations of the Cross to the Kapuziner Church on the hilltop.

The monastery church is very simply furnished. Its gothic main door dates from mid-15th century, with carved heads of prophets. Further up, a nature reserve is full of splendid lime and chestnut trees, a statue of Mozart and the sound of birds.

Otherwise, keep right of the church, and follow hikers' path no. 804. A little left turning points to "Stadtaussicht – Hettwer-Bastei". From this bastion you get superb panoramic views of the Old Town. Afterwards, steps lead down Imberg Stiege to Steingasse and thence to the river bank.

Museum of Natural History, Haus der Natur, Museumplatz 5. *See map, near fig. 13.*
A large exhibition of natural history, with an audio-visual show. Open daily 9-17 hrs, entrance AS 55.

Max Reinhard Memorial and Research Centre
Schloss Arenberg, Arenbergstrasse 10
This wonderful museum and study centre is dedicated to the great theatre director Max Reinhard, who founded the Salzburg Festival. Open: Mon-Fri 9-12 hrs daily. During the Festival open daily 10-17 hrs; during Mozart Week and Easter Festival open 11-16 hrs. Entrance: AS 40.

Salzburg Museum, Museumplatz 1. *Near fig. 13.*
Dedicated to history of Salzburg. Open: daily except Monday, 9-17 hrs. Entrance: AS 40.

Toy Museum, Bürgerspitalplatz 2. *See map fig. 12.*
A fascinating collection of old toys, applied art and musical instruments. Open: Tue-Sun 9-17 hrs. Entry AS 30.

Costume Museum, Griesgasse 23/1. *Near fig. 13.*
Displays traditional Salzburg costume. Open: Mon-Fri 10-12 and 14-17 hrs; Sat 10-12 hrs. Entrance AS 30.

3.6 Take a trip

On a brief City Break to Salzburg, try to schedule at least one afternoon to enjoy the city's supremely beautiful mountain setting. The wooded hills of Heuberg, Gaisberg and Untersberg are easily accessible by public transport, while the Salzkammergut region of lakes and mountains can best be sampled by coach tour. On a longer stay, add a trip into Germany – to Berchtesgaden where Hitler perched in his "Eagle's Nest".

There are two variations of Salzkammergut circuit. Very popular is the **Sound of Music** tour which combines some Salzburg sightseeing with two lakes – Fuschlsee and Mondsee – and the surrounding hills. The itinerary follows locations where the 1962 movie was filmed, and where the real-life Trapp family played out their personal story.

The regular **Salzkammergut Lakes and Mountains** tour features Lake Wolfgang, with time to explore the resort of St. Wolfgang, where the leading lakeside hotel was the model for the operetta *White Horse Inn*. This tour overlaps with the Sound of Music circuit, by stopping at the Collegiate Church in Mondsee, where the wedding scenes were filmed.

3.7 Sunday in Salzburg

All shops are closed Sundays, but most museums and restaurants are open, and sightseeing excursions are in full operation. There's always choice of musical events, morning, afternoon and evening. Mid-May till mid-August, for instance, there's an open-air promenade concert every Sunday in the Mirabell Garden 10.30-11.30 hrs.

There are regular services in the 38 Catholic churches of Salzburg. High Mass is both a religious and a musical experience – orchestra and choir 8.45 a.m. at the Franciscan Church; or with the splendid 4,000-pipe organ at 10 a.m. in the Cathedral. Listen to the greatest works of sacred music, performed in the original setting for which they were composed. There is only one Protestant church – facing Mirabell Garden on Schwarzstrasse.

3.8 Shopping

Salzburg is a treasure-house of high quality, traditional and often hand-made goods. Confectionery, Austrian glassware, petit-point handbags, candles and leather goods are typical products worth investigating.

Shop hours are Monday-Friday 8-18 hrs; Saturday 8-12 or 8-13 hrs. Many shops close for one or two hours at lunch. During the Festival many central shops stay open Saturday afternoon.

The most interesting shopping streets are in the heart of the old city – especially Getreidegasse, Judengasse and Griesgasse. Mainly they sell traditional items, clothes, chocolate, records and books. Across the river around Linzergasse shops tend to be more modern and cheaper, particularly the boutiques.

There's a good open-air market called Schrannenmarkt on Thursday mornings outside St. Andrew's Church on Mirabell Platz – fruit, flowers and veg.

3.9 Eating out in Salzburg

Buy a Packed Lunch

In fine weather it's delightful to picnic by the river or in Mirabell Gardens. Almost every supermarket and delicatessen can make up a 'Semmel' (bread roll) with the meat or cheese of your choice. Depending on the filling, reckon around AS 15.

A fruit and vegetable Green Market on Universitäts Platz is open Monday to Friday 6-19 hrs. It's worth a special visit on Saturdays till 13 hrs, when country folk from the Salzkammergut sell all kinds of home-made cakes, cheeses and other products.

Restaurants for lunch

Nordsee, Getreidegasse 27
Excellent seafood dishes and sandwiches to eat-in or take-away. Open 9-19 hrs; from June 1 till September 15, open till 23 hrs.

Shrimps Bar, Steingasse 5
Small, relaxed bar with tables outside on the cobbled Steingasse. Wide selection of seafood dishes. Open 11-23 hrs. Closed for two weeks' holiday in July.

Sternbräu, Griesgasse 23 – easily reached from Getreidegasse. A complex of restaurants. During summer months there's buffet-style service in the garden courtyard. Relaxed atmosphere with good food at reasonable prices. Open daily 8-24 hrs. Evening music on Fridays and Sundays.

McDonald's, on Getreidegasse
Although many people shudder at the idea, McDonald's can be ideal for a quick and cheap lunchtime snack. Open 9 hrs till around midnight.

Maria Plain, Maria Plain Kasern   Tel: 50701
Old mill situated next to a Pilgrimage church, on a hillside outside the city. Can be reached by bus or a no. 77 Lokalbahn from the Bahnhof, and a 20-minute country walk with a great panorama of the surrounding mountains of Salzburg, and of the city itself. Very good Austrian food, featuring local specialities. Closed Wednesdays.

For evening dining

Some time during your stay, try the well-known local speciality called Salzburger Nockerl – a super-light soufflé, very sweet. Order it early in the meal, as it takes half an hour to prepare. It arrives looking like three Salzburger mountain peaks, coloured yellow. A serving is plenty for two or three people.

See chapter 1.2 for a listing of other Austrian specialities.

Stieglbräu, Rainerstrasse 14   Tel: 877694
Hotel and restaurant belonging to the K&K chain. Has a large beer garden, with very good food and service.

K + K, Waagplatz 2 (just off Mozartplatz) Tel: 842156
Is slightly more expensive.

Priesterhausstube, Priesterhausgasse 12   Tel: 878317
Small and friendly with traditional decor. Excellent food and service, with big selection of Austrian and international dishes. Try the garlic snails!   Open daily except Monday, 17-01 hrs. Reservation advisable.

Zum fidelen Affen, Priesterhausgasse 8   Tel: 877361
Has been described as 'The Drunken Monkey', with a laid-back atmosphere. Popular with the locals, it's a place which one could visit alone and be guaranteed to feel welcome. Austrian food. Open 17-24 hrs, closed Sundays and throughout July.

Kobenzl, Gaisberg   Tel: 641510
For a very special occasion only!   This restaurant is in the most fantastic position – high above Salzburg with breathtaking views. Top quality cuisine including excellent Austrian dishes. You'll need taxis each way, adding to the high-cost meal. Reservations usually necessary. Closed Nov-Mar.

Schloss Mönchstein, Mönchsberg 26   Tel: 848555
An outstanding restaurant for a most special occasion, in a stunning location next to Café Winkler. In this converted castle you get very personal attention, and pay accordingly. Formal dress.

Reservation essential, as they have only about six tables. Nouvelle Cuisine.

Hagenauer Stuben, Universitätsplatz 14   Tel: 842657
A cosy candlelit restaurant with excellent Austrian food and wine. In summer you can eat outdoors next to a picturesque market.

Let your meal settle by wandering around the art exhibition on the upper floor, which usually features local contemporary artists. Closed Saturday afternoons and Sundays.

Zum Mohren, Judengasse 9   Tel: 842387
Historic building, very good Austrian and international cuisine. Reservations advised. Closed Sundays and all through November.

Wilder Mann, on Getreidegasse.   Tel: 841787
In a small courtyard, has lots of character, and is frequented especially by locals. Large portions. They do a
good Salzburger Nockerl.

Wienerwald, Griesgasse 31   Tel: 843470
Very good value, specialising in chicken dishes. Open 7-
24 hrs.

Stiftskeller St. Peter, St. Peterbezirk 1   Tel: 841268
Claims to be Austria's oldest restaurant, dating from 803.
Hot and cold snacks or a full meal in a medieval atmosphere, with outdoor eating and drinking at benches and
tables in the courtyard, or beneath the hollowed-out cliff.
Handily located below the Festung for people who have
been to a concert. Closed Mondays.

A short-list of cafés

*There are dozens of charming cafés all over Salzburg.
But here are a few favourites which are worth a special
visit – starting with a couple with special significance
for Mozart buffs.*

Café Glockenspiel
Very large, taking up an entire side of Mozart Square.
It's a good base for watching the tourist world go by,
and for listening to the Carillon at 11 a.m. or 6 p.m.

Tomaselli, Alter Markt 9
Traditional decor. Usually crowded with a good atmosphere. It was founded in 1703 by an Italian singer at the
court. He married a girl whose father had the original
license to serve coffee. Tomaselli gave up singing, and
opened the coffeeshop which is still operated by the same
family.
    When Mozart's wife was widowed, she married a
Danish diplomat who wrote the definitive biography of
Mozart. They lived in the flat above the café.

Bazar, Schwarzstrasse 3
An institution for the locals – everyone goes! Atmosphere
in abundance. Its riverside terrace offers a delightful
view across the Salzach. Closed Sundays.

Café Winkler – reached by lift up the Mönchsberg – is
very nice for a refreshment. Expensive, but you're also
paying for the view.

Hotel Stein, by the Stadtsbrücke
During July and August, Hotel Stein opens a rooftop café
with a fantastic view over the inner city.

3.10 Nightlife

Salzburg delights music-lovers not only during its world-
famed summer Festival. Concerts, theatre and folk events
are never out of season, and it's usually possible to get
tickets *somewhere*.

Around 15 official agencies sell tickets to all the main events at a standard 20% mark-up. Outside the big Festival season, programmes are mainly of chamber music. One of the pleasures is to hear these concerts in their original settings – not in a modern hall, but in the princely rooms where the performances were first given.

Best policy is to pick up the month's programme, published by the Salzburg Tourist Office, and go direct to the concert or theatre box office. As Salzburg is so small, it's really quite easy to drop by on your sightseeing rounds, and save the mark-up.

But don't just turn up on the night! Auditoriums are small, and all seats are normally filled. Try for the Salzburg Palace Concerts, which are held either at **Mirabell Palace** or at the **Residenz** next to the Cathedral. Similar performances are given at the **Festung**, where concerts are held in the splendid Fürstenzimmer from May till October. Seats are unnumbered. So, if you don't want a back seat, arrive 30 minutes early, when the doors open.

Other historic concert venues include the **Gothic Hall** of St. Blasius Church at the end of Getreidegasse, the **Mozarteum** on Schwarzstrasse, and out at **Hellbrunn Palace** for Mozart Serenades. Price range is AS 150-350.

Outside the Salzburg Festival season, live opera is infrequent except for some performances between mid-September and the first week of June at the **Landestheater**, close to the Mozarteum on Schwarzstrasse. Otherwise, opera-lovers should try the light-hearted alternative of the **Marionetten Theater** *(fig. 21)* next door.

To the recorded music of past Festival opera performances, life-size puppets perform in realistic style. The current repertoire of nine operas and operettas includes five works by Mozart. The marionettes' main Salzburg season runs April through September, including matinees during the Festival. They then rest for a month before departing on foreign tours. Prices are AS 350-450.

Salzburg Festival

For a dedicated music-lover, the Salzburg Festival is the dream of a lifetime. During the five-week season in July/August, the repertoire always includes at least six operas among the overall total of 130 performances in the full programme.

Ticket-buying demands advance planning! Especially for the big events, don't expect just to pick up tickets on arrival – though sometimes your friendly hotel concierge can oblige if you can face a huge mark-up. To buy tickets at cost price, here's the drill:

At the beginning of December, the Festival programme is published. Send for a copy from the ticket office in Salzburg – Kartenbüro der Salzburger Festspiele, Festspielhaus, A-5010 Salzburg. The programme contains an order form, for sending to the ticket office before the deadline of around January 7.

By the end of March, they will advise what tickets can be allocated. Then you must immediately settle the account, so the tickets can be despatched by registered post. If you miss that priority chance, just write later to the ticket office, in the hope of any seats left over from the first orders, or from cancellations.

The last chance is on-the-spot – first at the Festival box office, which is open Mon-Fri 9.30-17.00 hrs. There's also a ticket office called Polzer on Residenz Platz, next to the Cathedral, which handles returned tickets and cancellations.

If no luck, then go from one ticket agency to another. You may not get the seat or the performance of your dreams. But if you just want to participate in the Salzburg Festival – and every performance is superlative – then there's always chance of getting *something*.

Opera ticket prices start at 500 AS, and reach 4,000 AS. For concerts, reckon a range of 150-1500 AS. Dress is formal. For the prime occasions, such as Festival premieres, wear tails or dinner jacket; evening gown.

On the lighter side

Salzburg is not a city which explodes at night-time. It can be very quiet. Many visitors expect some Tyrolean-type oompah bands in restaurants. But that's not the Salzburg style, except for some evening folklore performances during summer months at the **Stiegel-Keller** at Festungsgasse 10, just below the fortress. *See map fig. 3.*

Folk-music and dance performances are also given during summer in the **Fortress Restaurant**.

Bars and clubs

For younger people, there are many good bars – tucked away, quite discreet. Bars along Giselakai are always popular, and clubs can be found off Neumayrplatz. For something different try the **Felsenkeller**, at Toscanini Hof by the Festspielhaus. Until midnight you can enjoy wine in a coin-studded cellar built right into the cliff.

Salzburg Casino operates daily from 3 p.m. till the small hours – French and American roulette, blackjack, one-arm bandits, and baccarat at weekends. They give you a starter kit of chips worth AS 200 for cut-price AS 170, and you also ride free on the lift. Take passport!

3.11 At your service

See also section 1.3 for information applicable to both Salzburg and Vienna – Currency, Phone Calls, Medical, News, Tipping, Austrian National Tourist Offices.

Money and Banking

Bank hours are Monday-Friday 8-12 and 14-16.30 hrs. Exchange Bureau at Main Railway Station – 7-22 hrs.

Bankhaus Daghofer at Griesgasse 11 is also open Sat 8.30-17 hrs, and Sun 9-16 hrs.
Rieger Bank, Judengasse 13 is also open Sat 9.30-14 hrs, and on Sundays during the Festival 10-15 hrs.
In July/August, exchange offices are likewise open Sat and Sun at the Tourist Information Centre in Mozart Square, and at the Fortress funicular exchange office. The exchange office at Alter Markt opens Sat 9.30-12 hrs July to September.

Post and Telephone
Main Post Office with Poste Restante service:
Residenplatz 9. Open: Mon-Fri 7-19 hrs; Sat 8-10 hrs.

Calls to UK: see Vienna chapter, Section 2.11.

Emergency phone numbers
Police – 133; Fire 122; Ambulance 144.

Should you have anything stolen, you must report it to the Police for insurance purposes, whereupon you will be issued with a declaration.
Police HQ & Lost Property, Rudolfplatz 3 Tel: 642804

Medical
For information on the nearest general practitioner, specialist or dentist: Ärztekammer für Salzburg, Schrannengasse 2 – Tel: 871327. Doctor or Dentist, Information Sat, Sun and Public Holidays only – 141.
Emergency Centre, Paris-Lodron-Strasse 8a   Tel: 141
Open: Sat 7 a.m. till Mon 7 a.m. and public holidays
Pharmaceutical Chemists
General Opening: Mon-Fri 8-12 and 14.30-18 hrs; Sat 8-12 hrs.
Night and Sunday service: If closed, shops display a list of nearest night chemist.
Hospitals
Accident Hospital: Dr Franz-Rehrl-Platz 5   Tel: 6580
Hospital of the Barmherzigen Brüder, Kajetanerplatz 1
Tel: 844531
Dentists
Österreich Dentistenkammer, Faberstrasse 2 Tel: 843777

Consulates
UK, Alter Markt 4   Tel: 848133
USA, Giselakai 51   Tel: 28601

Salzburg Tourist Office
For information, maps or brochures on Salzburg or the surrounding area, contact the very helpful Tourist Office at Mozartplatz 5.   Tel: 847568
There's also an Information Office at the Railway Station on Platform 2   Tel: 871712

Market Square and Tyn Church, Prague

Charles Bridge, Prague

St. Nicholas Dome as seen from the Charles Bridge

Schönbrunn Palace, Vienna

Prater Fun Fair, Vienna

Johann Strauss statue, Vienna

Views over Salzburg

Cloth Hall, Krakow

Krakow Cathedral

Old town square, Warsaw

Fisherman's Bastion, Budapest

A famous Hungarian landmark, the Chain Bridge

Chapter Four

Prague

4.1 City of dreaming spires

Prague ranks high among the more beautiful capitals of Europe, and happily was relatively untouched by two World Wars. Sited on the River Vltava – itself a lyrical theme for painters and musicians – it's a city of a hundred spires that dominate the skyline.

There's enough to keep a sightseer busy for several days. Prague abounds in picturesque old streets that wind up steep cobbled hillsides, with Hradčany Castle as the highlight. Palaces are preserved as museums. There is plentiful mixture of Baroque, Gothic and Renaissance architecture.

For many years, owing to other priorities, Prague had a dilapidated, run-down appearance. But in more recent times public buildings have been given a major face-lift. The blackened grime of past decades has been scrubbed away, to reveal the beautiful pastel colours of the original stonework. The clean-up continues.

By night, Prague offers good opportunities for opera and ballet, orchestral and chamber music, puppet shows. Leading hotels feature Western-style night-clubs and dancing, with reasonable prices unless you order drinks imported from hard-currency countries.

For a quieter drink, there are some elegant bars with suave service. At the other extreme are noisy smoke-filled beer taverns and cellars where devotees weigh up the merits of the great variety of different brews.

Prague is a good base for excursions through a countryside of tranquil rivers, pine-clad hills, historic castles and picture-book farmhouses and villages, well-painted and trim. Smetana's tone-poem "Má Vlast" (My Country) gives a musical picture of Bohemia's serenity, little changed by the 20th century.

Many castles are located in the area. Among the finest is Hluboká. Sited 250 feet above the Vltava, it is modelled on England's Windsor Castle, and contains a superb collection of tapestry, furniture and arms.

Expenses on meals, transport and entertainment are extremely low when calculated at current exchange rates.

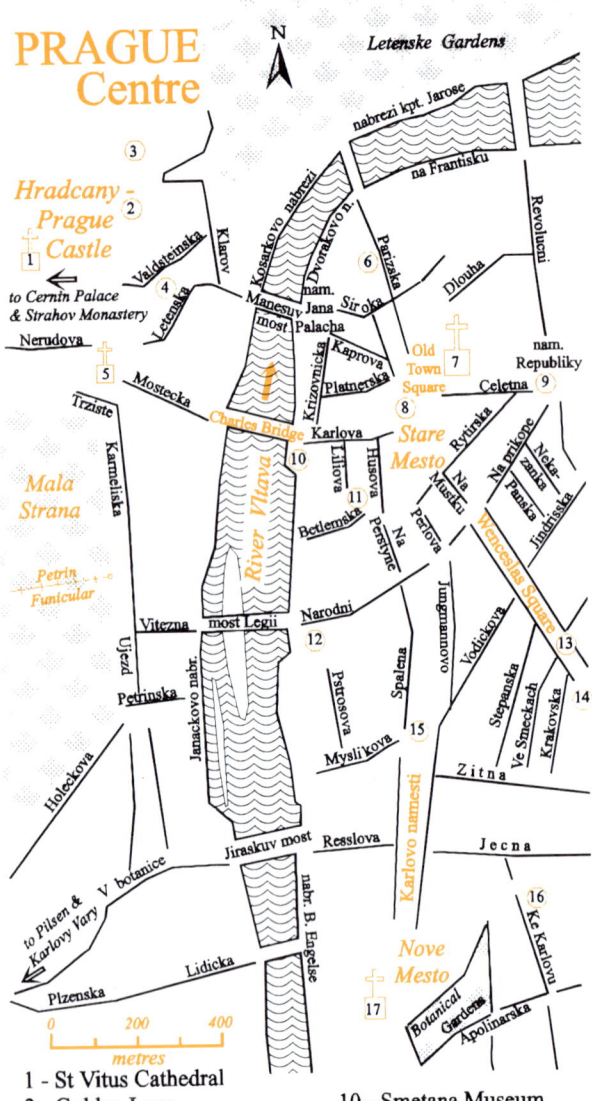

PRAGUE Centre

Letenske Gardens

N

Hradcany - Prague Castle

to Cernin Palace & Strahov Monastery

nabrezi kpt. Jarose

na Frantisku

Revolucni

Klarov

Valdsteinska

Letenska

Nerudova

Mostecka

Trziste

Karmeliska

Mala Strana

Petrin Funicular

Vitezna

Ujezd

Petrinska

Holeckova

to Pilsen & Karlovy Vary

V botanice

Plzenska

Lidicka

Kosarkovo nabrezi

Dvorakovo n.

Manesuv most

nam. Jana Palacha

Parizska

Siroka

nam. Republiky

Dlouha

Krizovnicka

Kaprova

Platnerska

Karlova

Lilova

Husova

Betlemska

Na perstyne

Na prikope

Jungmannovo

Celetna

Rytirska

Na Mustku

Na prikope

Panska

Jindrisska

Nekaz anka

Wenceslas Square

Stepanska

Vodickova

Ve Smeckach

Krakovska

Stare Mesto

Old Town Square

Charles Bridge

River Vltava

most Legii

Narodni

Petrova

Na

Spalena

Perstova

Myslikova

Jiraskuv most

Resslova

Karlovo namesti

Zitna

J e c n a

Ke Karlovu

Nove Mesto

Botanical Gardens

Apolinarska

Janackovo nabr.

nabr. B. Engelse

0   200   400
metres

1 - St Vitus Cathedral
2 - Golden Lane
3 - Royal Summer Palace
4 - Waldstein Palace Gardens
5 - St Nicholas Church
6 - Historic Ghetto
7 - Tyn Church
8 - Old Town Hall & Clock
9 - Powder Tower

10 - Smetana Museum
11 - Bethlehem Chapel
12 - National Theatre
13 - Wenceslas Monument
14 - National Museum
15 - New Town Hall
16 - Dvorak Museum
17 - Emmaus Monastery

Market economy

After the dramatic political events of December 1989, moves towards a market economy changed many of the former subsidised prices. Exchange rates have kept remarkably stable. Room tariffs at hotels are closer to Western levels, but visitors will probably continue to enjoy low-level expenses, with all the fascination of seeing Prague under new management.

Since January 1993, the Czech Republic and Slovakia have been independent of each other – no longer joined together as Czechoslovakia.

4.2 Arrival & hotel

By air, London Heathrow to Prague is served daily by either British Airways or Czech Airlines. For two-centre travellers, there are daily flights from Vienna by Czech Airlines or Austrian Airlines. By train from Vienna's Franz Josef Bahnhof takes 5½ hours, or about the same by motor-coach. There are likewise good air connections with Budapest or Warsaw.

Visas for British passport-holders have been abolished since 1990. However, if you wish to contact the Czech Republic Embassy, the address is 28 Kensington Palace Gardens, London W8 4QY – Tel: 0171-293 1115.

There is a Czech Centre at the Embassy – Tel: 0171-243 7981. The London office of Čedok is specialised in business travel.

In Prague, Čedok is still the largest travel organisation, but many competing agencies have opened since 1991. Thomson's local agents are Cityrama, at Stěpanská 21, 11000 Prague. Tel: 24911122; Fax: 24911128. Their office and reps are available for any advice or information you may require whilst in Prague. They provide a currency exchange service, and can book any of the excursions available.

Airport transfer

If you are making your own way to or from the airport, expect to pay about £2 by airport bus to the city centre for a journey time of about 30 minutes; or around £10 by taxi. Be sure to agree the price first, as some drivers are more than ready to take advantage of visitors.

Hotel grades can compare with those of West-European countries, but rooms are in short supply owing to the popularity of Prague as a tourist destination.

In the centre, elderly hotels like the Ambassador, Esplanade and Palace have been modernised, while keeping their traditional atmosphere. Indeed, the art-deco Palace Hotel has been totally rebuilt inside the original facade, and has moved up to luxury grade.

With a basic policy of preserving the historic appearance of the city centre, the modern international style of

high-rise glass and concrete has been kept a decent distance away. The Inter-Continental on the river bank does
not obtrude, and the high-rise Forum Praha is several
Metro stops away from the centre. Three botels are
moored by the river bank to help ease the bed shortage.
Several other hotels have recently opened, and more are
under construction.

4.3 Getting around Prague

Public transport

Most of the city hotels are within easy stroll of the tourist areas, or just a few stops on the clean and modern
Metro system. Visitors need make very little use of public transport, which operates between 5 a.m. and midnight every day.

Elderly trams trundle and clank to all corners of
Prague, with numerous bus services as a back-up. Ticket
prices have increased, but are still incredibly low – the
same price regardless of distance. On a three-day visit,
it's hard to spend more than a pound or two on inner-city
transport.

Buses and trams

Your hotel staff or tour rep will give advice on direct
bus and tram routes, which are easy to use. Tickets must
be bought in advance from hotel receptions, tobacconists,
newsagents and Metro stations. There are no conductors,
so you must punch your own ticket. Don't forget, as
there are occasional controls. Anyone without a validated
ticket gets an on-the-spot fine. Use a fresh ticket each
time you change.

Metro

The standard fare covers the entire journey, regardless of
any changes. There are three lines:

A – which runs East to West
B and C – which both run North to South.

At the subway, the same tickets are used as for buses
and trams.

To plan your route, look for the last station on the
line. This gives you the name of the line to follow.

Look for the words VSTUP = Entrance; VÝSTUP =
Exit.

Taxis

Cheap but elusive! Radio cabs can take ages to arrive.
During the day, taxis are more prevalent and often lurk
near the big hotels, where they hope to pick up hard-
currency passengers. If you need a taxi late at night,
check how much the journey will cost, and even haggle!

Taxi meters don't always work for foreign visitors.

Car Hire

Rented cars are now available through most of the international hire companies. Here are some contacts:

Avis – Klimentska 46, Prague 1. Tel: 21851225; Airport: 20114270 or 3166739.

Hertz – at Airport; and in Charles Square Tel: 2901122.

Europcar – Tel: 3167849.

Czechocar – Palace of Culture Tel: 61222079.

4.4 Basic Prague

Most of sightseeing Prague is comfortably within walking distance. On a short visit, the following check-list covers the highlights.

(1) Explore Hradčany Castle and the Golden Lane of the medieval alchemists. *See map figs. 1 & 2.*

(2) Take a trip by paddle steamer on the Vltava.

(3) On the hour, see and hear the performance of the medieval clock on the Old Town Hall *(see map fig. 8).*

(4) Saunter along Charles Bridge among the craft workers and entertainers.

(5) Inspect Bohemia crystal and Carlsbad porcelain at high-grade shops on Na příkopě and Celetná Street.

(6) Wander at random into ancient courtyards and alleys in the central area around the Old Town Hall Square.

(7) For a most unusual theatre experience, try to get tickets for the 'Laterna Magika' show.

(8) Pay homage at the informal memorial to Jan Palach in Wenceslas Square. *See map fig. 13.*

(9) Sample different brews at the U Fleků beer-house.

(10) Enjoy an out-of-town coach excursion to see historic castles and the beautiful Czech countryside.

Orientation

Sightseers' Prague comprises four main centres of attraction on the city map – two on each side of the River Vltava which flows through the capital. Eight river islands are mostly used for sporting activities.

Dominating the skyline is the **Hradčany** district: the Castle, several aristocratic palaces, the tall silhouette of St. Vitus Cathedral and a delightful Golden Lane *(map fig. 2)* that was an R&D centre for medieval alchemists.

At the foot of the Hradčany complex is **Malá Strana**, the Lesser Town: a Prague Baroque district of 17th- and 18th-century mansions and embassies, with the Jesuit St Nicholas Church *(map fig. 5)* overlooking the central square called Malostranské náměstí. Traditional coffee-houses and restaurants are numerous in this area, which is also a principal stopping-point for buses and trams.

Out of the fifteen bridges which cross the Vltava, the tourist favourite is the 14th-century Charles Bridge, one of Europe's oldest and most decorative stone bridges.

Old and New Towns

Directly opposite Charles Bridge is **Karlova Street**, lined with splendid town houses and winding towards the Town Hall Square (Staroměstské náměstí), which is the fabulous centrepiece of Staré Město or Old Town. Down the wide Paris Street (Pařížská) leads back to the river at the Intercontinental Hotel. Close by is the former ghetto which includes the oldest existing synagogue in Europe: one of the buildings which forms part of the Jewish National Museum. Another direction from the Town Hall Square leads along Celetná Street to the Powder Tower (*fig. 9*). This was the Royal Road taken by Bohemian kings when they went in state procession to Prague Castle.

Powder Tower stands at one end of Na příkopě, the lively shopping street which follows the line of the former moat between Old and New Towns. At the other end of Na příkopě, where it meets the lower end of Wenceslas Square, was the scene of the demonstrations of November 1989 which led to collapse of Communist government. *See map fig. 13.*

The New Town is the principal area of shops, restaurants and hotels.

All four areas are pedestrianized, so that sightseeing on foot is a jay-walker's paradise. You can easily link up Prague's highlights with almost nil possibility of being stabbed in the back by a Škoda motor-car.

Castle district, Hradčany

By public transport, take a tram or Metro to Malostranská, then tram 22 uphill to Hradčany and follow the crowds to Hradčanské náměstí. Sightseeing is then downhill all the way.

Located in the Castle district are three major sites: Strahov Monastery, Černín Palace and the Loreta. In their eagerness to reach the Castle itself, many individuals and groups pass them by. If possible, schedule time to see them more closely another day.

Strahov Monastery was founded in 1140, and is famed for its superb baroque library. The rich collection forms part of the **Museum of Czech Literature** and includes works by Jan Hus and his followers. Open daily 9.30-17.00 hrs.

Close by on **Loretto Square** (Loretánské nám.) is the long facade of **Černín Palace**, founded in 17th century but largely rebuilt about 60 years ago to house the Ministry of Foreign Affairs. In 1948, Jan Masaryk (the Foreign Minister, and son of the country's first president) fell or was pushed to his death from one of the windows.

Across the square is the **Loretto Shrine**, which has been a major place of pilgrimage for centuries. There's much interest in the baroque facade, the cloisters (lined with painted saints), the central Santa Casa chapel, the Loretto Treasury and the Church of the Nativity.

Hradčany Square

This elegant square was centre of the original Hradčany town, and has retained its basic medieval layout. Around the approach to Prague Castle are mansions and palaces, mostly 16th century Renaissance style.

On the right, at No. 2 next to St. Benedict's Church, is the mid-16th century **Schwarzenberg Palace** which today houses the Museum of Military History. No. 5 is Tuscany Palace with an Early Baroque facade. No. 1 is Salm Palace, now the Swiss Embassy.

Walk towards the Castle gates, but first diverge to the right for a superb viewpoint over the city.

Prague Castle, Hradčany

Enter the ceremonial gates into Prague Castle, founded in the 9th century. A Romanesque palace was built on the site in the 12th century, and has been rebuilt or reconstructed several times since. In 14th century the Castle became a royal residence, but later served mainly as a centre of government.

With establishment of the Czechoslovak Republic in 1918, Hradčany became the President's official seat. President Václav Havel has moved in, after an initial period when he chose not to live in the Castle, but in his private home. Reception rooms are used for State occasions and are not open to the public.

Cathedral of St. Vitus

In the third courtyard of Prague Castle stands the cathedral, founded in year 926. *See map fig. 1.* The present Gothic building dates from 14th century, and was designed by a French architect. The steeple was completed in 1562, while the Baroque roof dates from 1770. Final completion of the cathedral was in 1929.

Something like the Westminster Abbey of Prague, St. Vitus Cathedral has been the setting for all big State occasions, the burial place of princes and kings, and the treasury for the Bohemian crown jewels.

Good King Wenceslas – St. Václav – is buried in the Wenceslas Chapel, which was constructed between 1347 and 1366. He was the good king who helped spread Christianity during his reign from 920-929. He was then assassinated by his brother, who disliked the mixing of religion with practical politics.

The martyred King Wenceslas later became the patron saint of Bohemia, and is the favourite symbol today of Czech unity against foreign influence. His chapel is decorated with frescoes and semi-precious stones.

Vikářská Street

Along the north side of the Cathedral is the narrow but charming Vikářská Street, which has changed little from past centuries. The Vikárka restaurant and wine tavern is housed in the former Old and New Vicarages, which adjoin the Old Deanery. The restaurant is partly built into the Castle fortifications.

St. George's Basilica

Behind the Cathedral is George Square with a splendid basilica founded in 920 and completed in the 12th century. St. George's Basilica is the best-preserved Romanesque building in Bohemia.

Golden Lane – Zlatá ulička

Further down, reached by a little turning to the left, is the favourite tourist haunt of Golden Lane – one of Prague's most popular photo targets. *See map fig. 2.* It's a group of tiny medieval houses which formerly were the haunt of alchemists, trying to turn base metal into gold. They have been converted into enticing little shops that transmute souvenirs and antiques into hard currency.

The Lesser Town – Malá Strana

Walking down from Prague Castle brings you into the Malá Strana district of town mansions, picturesque side streets and Prague Baroque monuments. Centre of the district is Malostranské náměstí. Many of the buildings have dingy and crumbling facades, but work continues to restore them to their original colourful condition.

New Town Hall, Malostranské náměstí

Of the original Gothic structure, only the cellars and double colonnade of the ground floor have been preserved.

St. Nicholas Church, Malostranské náměstí

The most outstanding example of Bohemian Baroque in Prague, completed in 1755. Open: 9-16 hrs. *Map fig. 5.*

Charles Bridge

Charles Bridge must rate very high among the top ten tourist-interest bridges of Europe. A pedestrian bridge, highly popular with visitors and residents alike, it offers delight in all seasons. The bridge is named after Charles 1V, greatest of the Czech kings.

Viewpoints and photo possibilities open up almost everywhere you look. Dating from 1357, the bridge parapets are lined with thirty Baroque statues and groups which were added in early 18th century. Buskers and craft peddlers crowd the bridge, end to end. On fine summer days, it can easily take half an hour to work past all the distractions.

Caution: when the bridge is very crowded, it becomes an ideal workplace for professional pickpockets. Take care!

The Old Town – Staré Město

Focal point of the historic trading centre of Prague is the **Old Town Square** – Staroměstské náměstí – which originated in 10th century as a broad marketplace. In the middle of the cobbled expanse is a very large monument to John Huss – Jan Hus – the Czech religious reformer who was greatly influenced by England's John Wycliffe.

The surrounding steps offer a good viewpoint, with the chance of sitting down to absorb the fabulous setting.

Dominating the square are the twin towers of **Tyn Church** – an Early Gothic triple-naved building that dates mainly from mid-14th century. For years it was wrapped in scaffolding while renovations continued; but entry is now possible. *See map fig. 7.*

Just before every hour through the day, crowds congregate outside the Old Town Hall, to see a performance of the **Astronomical Clock**. *See map fig. 8.*

Built by a master watchmaker in 1410, it's the oldest of its kind in Europe to be still operating. Two upper windows open on the stroke of every hour, to unleash a procession of the 12 apostles. Below the windows is an astronomical sphere which indicates the three different times used in the Middle Ages. Standing on each side are figures representing human vanity and miserliness, a skeleton and the figure of a Turk.

Caution: amid the tightly packed crowds who gather every hour, there'll usually be a pickpocket or two!

From the Town Hall's arched entrance alongside, wedding parties surge out at intervals from their civil ceremonies. Horse-carriage rides start from the other side.

Events

Year-round there's always something happening in the Old Town Square, making it a great meeting-place. In midsummer craft workers give on-the-spot demonstrations; or possibly a historical fencing group will give a theatrical display against a backdrop of the pastel-coloured buildings. In December the square is setting for a traditional Christmas market.

The square and its surrounding streets and courtyards are well supplied with cafés, restaurants and ale-houses, making it a delightful area for an evening stroll by gaslight in search of food and refreshment.

Each of the radiating streets leads to other points of interest in the Old Town. The little square of Malé náměstí funnels into Karlova, which goes direct to Charles Bridge.

Melantrichova or Železná Streets take you through to Wenceslas Square and Na příkopě. Celetná is the superbly reconstructed Royal Road leading to the Powder Tower. Pařížská – a street of airline offices – goes to the old Jewish ghetto area and to the Intercontinental Hotel.

Na příkopě

Na příkopě came into existence only in the 18th century, when the Old Town moat was filled in. Covering the short distance between the Powder Tower and Wenceslas Square, Na příkopě has been greatly improved by the removal of tram lines and opening of a pedestrian precinct.

Good shops, restaurants and cafés have made this into the liveliest of Prague streets. Several pavement cafés operate in summer, with moderate prices.

In this area you can also experience the old-time coffeehouse scene. By the **Powder Tower** (*see map fig. 9*), Na příkopě opens into a square called Náměstí Republiky. The next building is Obecní dům – Municipal House – which features a very large traditional Kavárna, with outdoor seating in fine weather.

Inside is more interesting, where you can sample a fattening range of ices and cream cakes in a late 19th-century setting, art nouveau style. As part of the complex of concert halls and meeting rooms, there's also a large restaurant, a basement wine cellar, and a Rock Club.

Wenceslas Square – Václavské náměstí

Over half a mile long and seventy yards wide, Wenceslas Square has flourished as the town's principal thoroughfare, shopping and social centre, ever since Charles 1V founded the New Town in 1348. At first it was called Horse Market, but the name was changed to Wenceslas Square in 1848 – though the Good King's present statue was not erected until 1912. *See map fig. 13.*

Like Na příkopě, Wenceslas Square has been greatly improved in recent years by banishing tramcars and converting most of the boulevard into a pedestrian precinct. With so many windows for shop-gazing, sedate hotels and intriguing arcades and courtyards, it's certainly worth exploring both sides of the avenue.

Well-tended flower displays line the central promenade. At the top end the National Museum (*see map fig. 14*) dominates the background to St. Wenceslas. Just below the statue has become a place of political pilgrimage. An informal shrine is dedicated to Jan Palach, the student who burned himself to death in protest at Soviet occupation. His photograph – and those of other leaders from the Republic's recent history – is always surrounded by fresh flowers and burning candles.

4.5 Other sights and monuments

Prague Ghetto (Old Jewish quarter) – located in streets around Široká and Pařížská, near Intercontinental Hotel. A few monuments have survived from the old Prague ghetto, including the early Gothic synagogue.

State Jewish Museum, 3 Jáchymova.
The objects displayed were collected by the Nazis.
Open: 9-16 hrs. Closed: Saturday.

Bethlehem Chapel, Betlemské náměstí, Prague 1.
Gothic Chapel completed in 1391. The Czech religious reformer John Huss preached here in the years 1402-13. Open: 9-18 hrs (April-September); 9-17 hrs (October). Closed: November-March. *See map fig. 11.*

Powder Tower – Prašná brána, Celetná Street
Gothic tower built 1475. It's the only tower remaining from the original fortifications of Prague Old Town. Views over central Prague are well worth the effort of climbing three lots of narrow spiral stairs. However, the tower may be closed for renovation. *See map fig. 9.*

Royal Summer Palace – Královský letohrádek, Belvedere. *See map fig. 3.*
Renaissance palace built in 1535-1563. The gardens contain a bronze 'singing fountain' cast in 1568. Open: Daily except Monday, 10-18 hrs. Closed during winter.

The Clementinum, Křížovnické nám. 4
A Baroque building dating from mid-17th century. Originally a Jesuit college, it now houses the Czech State Library.

Museums and Galleries

National Museum, Václavské náměstí 68. *Map fig. 14.*
Dominating the top end of Wenceslas Square: the oldest museum in Prague, housing geological, zoological, prehistoric, historic and cultural collections.
Open: 9-17 hrs. Closed: first Tuesday of the month.

National Technology Museum, Kostelní 42, Prague 7
Exhibition of Czech technology.
Open: 9-17 hrs. Closed: Monday

Museum of Decorative Arts, 17. listopadu 2.
This turn-of-the-century Neo-Renaissance building houses one of the world's largest glass and porcelain collections, from 14th-century Bohemian glass onwards. Also contains a vast collection of 30,000 posters, and Applied Art of the 16th-19th centuries.
Open: Tue-Sun 10-18 hrs.

Slightly off-trail
One of the current 'problems' of Prague is the congestion around the principal sites mentioned in the previous section – Basic Prague. The city tourist authorities are actively tackling this problem by renovating more of Prague's wealth of palaces, historic buildings, churches

and museums. These additional attractions are helping to smooth out the flow of sightseers.

Only just off the main tourist trail, in the Malá Strana (Lesser Town) district that sits on the slopes between the river and Prague Castle, are the **Waldstein Gardens and Palace** (*map fig. 4*), on Valdštejnské náměstí. This is one of the finest Baroque-style palaces in Prague, built 1623-1630. From May to September the gardens are open Tue-Sun through an entrance in Letenská Street, 10-18 hrs.

New Town centre

Another area worth exploring is around **Charles Square** – Karlovo náměstí – which is laid out as a park. Here is the centre of New Town (Nové Město), dating from the 12th century. At the north end stands the **New Town Hall** (*see map fig. 15*) which in 1419 was the scene of Prague's first defenestration, when councillors were thrown out the window by Hussite followers of the Reformation.

Halfway down Charles Square, Resslova Street leads to the river past the baroque church of **St Cyril and St Methodius**. The pock-marked walls bear witness to the battle that took place in 1942, when German SS troops massacred over 120 underground Czech fighters following the assassination of the notorious SS chief Heydrich.

At the southern end of Charles Square is the **Faust House** (Faustův Dům), a 16th-century palace which acquired its present baroque facade in mid-18th century. Several alchemists lived here, including an English trickster named Edward Kelley.

Continue south along Vyšehradská to reach **Emmaus Monastery** – Klášter Emauzy on Na Slovanech. *See map fig. 17.* This former monastery of the Slavonic Benedictines was founded in mid-14th century, and had a mixed-up career over the centuries. Badly damaged by bombing in 1945, it was tastefully reconstructed during the 1960's.

Close by are the **Botanical Gardens** (Botanická zahrada), noted for rhododendrons and azaleas. Open daily.

Also in this area, music-lovers should find their way to the Michna Summer Palace at Ke Karlovu 20, where the newly restored **Antonín Dvořák Museum** is dedicated to the composer's life. Open: Tue-Sun 10-17 hrs. *See map fig. 16.*

4.6 Take a trip

There is great beauty in the Czech countryside – rolling hills, woodlands, tiny villages and scattered farmhouses. Within one-day touring range are historic castles which add great sightseeing interest to the scenic pleasures, especially southwards. By rented car you can explore the region, or choose from a selection of coach tours.

Into the countryside

Karlštejn – 20 miles out from Prague, along the Vltava and Berounka valleys. In a magnificent forest setting, the Bohemian Gothic castle was founded in 1348 by Charles IV to guard the royal treasures and crown jewels. It rates as one of the Czech Republic's most important monuments.

Slapy Lake – a blissful recreational area created by Slapy dam on the River Vltava. There are direct buses from Prague.

Konopiště – Long avenues of trees lead to this castle which was almost totally rebuilt from 1887 by Archduke Franz Ferdinand, heir to the Austrian throne and later assassinated at Sarajevo.

The Duke was dedicated to hunting, and kept a detailed account-book of his lifetime's 300,000 bag, with sub-totals for every species of animal or bird. Large numbers of the trophies fill the walls. The castle also houses a great collection of arms from 15th and 16th centuries.

Orlík – A dam on the Vltava has created a 40-mile lake, very popular for canoeists and fishermen. Two castles can be visited: the Gothic-style hunting castle of Orlík and the medieval Bohemian royal castle of Zvíkov.

České Budějovice and Hluboká Castle – A historic town 90 miles due south of Prague, on the Vltava. Its magnificent central square is among the largest in Europe. Home of Budweiser beer and Koh-I-Noor pencils. Four miles north is the romantic chateau of Hluboká, rebuilt last century in the style of Windsor Castle.

In other directions, excursion possibilities include a beer connoisseur's visit to Pilsen, visiting the Urquell Brewery; to the spa town of Karlovy Vary (former Karlsbad) in the woodlands of West Bohemia; or eastwards to the medieval silver-mining town of Kutná Hora.

4.7 Sunday in Prague

Prague has a great musical tradition which is reflected in the choral music of its many churches. Specially recommended is to attend a service at the magnificent 14th-century Tyn Church (*see map fig. 7*) on the Old Town Square. Even more historic is the Cathedral of St. Vitus, founded in 10th century. *See map fig. 1*. In this devout Roman Catholic country, congregations are large.

All Prague museums are open on Sunday (mostly closed Monday). Shops, banks and offices are firmly closed.

Several out-of-town excursions operate on Sundays, which can be a good day for sightseeing of castles and countryside around the capital, when the locals also are out there enjoying themselves.

4.8 Shopping in Prague

As the Czech Republic moves towards a market economy, it's hard to predict how price levels will change. For the City Break visitor, part of the background interest comes from seeing how a country transforms from one social system to another.

The main shopping areas are in the streets radiating from the Old Town Square and around Wenceslas Square. On Celetná Street are most of the quality stores which sell music recordings and CD's, crystal glass, Jablonec costume jewelry and women's wear. Several beautiful shops along Na příkopě and neighbouring streets sell the famous coloured and cut glass, and porcelain.

It's fascinating to go window-shopping and pricing the goods along Wenceslas Square, which includes a number of food stores. Many prices may seem remarkably low. At the Supraphon music stores, for instance, reckon classical CD's at £3 each. Czech wine from Southern Moravia is usually a good buy, as are the smoked meats and chocolates.

The Republic has good reputation for leather, and shoes especially are reasonably priced, though of 'sensible' style rather than high fashion. In Wenceslas Square there is enormous choice of footwear at No. 6 – the blue and white Baťa building, which has several floors entirely devoted to shoes of every description.

In Na příkopě, the department store called Dětský Dům caters entirely for children – clothes, toys and the like. In many stores of the serve-yourself type, the number of customers is restrained by the number of wire baskets available. Shops are open 8-19 hrs Mon-Fri; 8-14 hrs Sat. Closed Sundays.

4.9 Eating out in Prague

Recent years have seen a boom in the Prague restaurant scene. Compared with the former limited choice, there are now hundreds of restaurants, bars and taverns.

Czechs are hearty eaters who scorn the rigours of health food and nouvelle cuisine. Typical meals are built around dumplings and sauerkraut, especially with pork or young goose. Fruit dumplings are popular, filled with plums, apricots, strawberries or cherries. Particularly good is Prague ham, which also can appear at breakfast. For Christmas dinner – traditionally eaten on Christmas Eve – the main course is poached carp: a freshwater fish which appears year-round on lunch and dinner menus.

In the international-grade restaurants you can expect an excellent meal for £15 or less, including wine. In average restaurants £10 can easily cover a good 3-course meal. People in Prague eat early, and dining rooms close earlier than in other Continental capitals. Don't get caught out!

During summer, restaurants stay open longer, but in winter they are tightly closed by 23 hrs. All restaurants follow a 'No Smoking' policy during the busiest hours of midday till 2 p.m., and around 7 p.m. Outside those peak hours, smoking may be permitted.

Numerous cafés are scattered all over Prague, serving a variety of cakes, rolls and drinks. Shop items like canned beer, picnic supplies or ice-cream cornets are unbelievably cheap. Stand-up self-service cafés offer very low-cost snacks, and are usually crowded.

If you prefer sitting down, the most famous cafés are clustered on Wenceslas Square (Václavské náměstí) and other central locations. Try the cafés attached to hotels such as the Ambassador, Jalta or the Europe, and enjoy the more leisured ambiance. Look for the word *Kaváma*.

Many restaurant menus are duplicated into German and English. Otherwise, how to read the menu, if there are no clues? Here's a basic guide to Czech cuisine.

Soups and Starters

Bramborová	Potato soup
Gulášová	Goulash soup
Hovězí	Beef broth
Pražská šunka	Prague ham
Ruské vejce	Egg mayonnaise
Uherský salám	Hungarian salami
Zeleninová	Vegetable soup

Main courses

Hovězí maso	Beef
Husa	Goose
Játra	Liver
Kachna	Duck
Karbanátky	Hamburgers
Kuře	Chicken
Pstruh	Trout
Rybí filet	Fish fillet
Telecí maso	Veal
Vepřové maso	Pork

Vegetables and Salads

Brambory	Potatoes
Bramborový salát	Potato salad
Hlávkový salát	Lettuce
Hrášek	Green peas
Knedlíky	Dumplings
Mrkev	Carrots
Okurkový salát	Cucumber
Rajčatový salát	Tomato
Rýže	Rice
Špenát	Spinach

Vegetarian dishes

Zelenina	Vegetables
Vejce	Eggs
Knedlíky s vejci	Dumplings with scrambled eggs
Smažený sýr	Fried cheese

Fruit and Desserts

Broskev	Peach
Dort	Cake, gateau
Hrušky	Pears
Jablka	Apple
Švestky	Plums
Třešně	Cherries
Ovocné knedlíky	Fruit dumplings
Meruňka	Apricot
Šlehačka	Whipped cream

Drinks

Čaj	Tea
Káva	Coffee
Minerálka	Mineral water
Mléko	Milk
Ovocná šťáva	Fruit juice
Pivo	Beer
Slivovice	Plum brandy, burns with a blue flame.
Víno	Wine
Vinný střik	Wine with soda water

Among the prime Czech specialities to sample are:
• Svíčková na smetaně s brusinkami a knedlíky – fillet of beef in cream sauce with cranberries and dumplings.
• Vepřo, knedlo, zelo – roast pork, dumplings, sauerkraut.
• Bramborák – potato pancakes with bacon, sausage, garlic and marjoram.
• Pečená husa s knedlíkem – roast goose with dumplings.
• Hovězí guláš – beef goulash.
• Švestkové knedlíky – sweet plum dumplings

Beer and wine

The generally heavy, savoury food goes down best of all with cold Czech beer, a brew admired for centuries by experts everywhere. Try some Pilsner, or Budvar (Budweiser), Staropramen, Bráník, or Velké Popovice. Part of the enjoyment comes from sampling the product in traditional taverns.

If you are not keen on beer, then try the Moravian and Czech wines, either in a regular restaurant of in a dedicated wine-tavern. The best appetiser is a typical Czech liquor called Becherovka, which can even serve as a digestive.

Restaurant guide

All the leading hotels feature excellent international cuisine. For a high-grade meal in luxury surroundings, try the first-floor restaurant at the Palace Hotel.

On Celetná Street in the Old Town are some very pleasing restaurants, cafés and wine-bars, several in delightful courtyards. There is a vegetarian restaurant called Vegetárka on the first floor of No. 3 Celetná. Opposite, at No. 2, is the vinárna u Sixtů, with an attractive modern-style café on the ground floor, and a wine-cellar below which stays open till 1 a.m. The entire central area can now feature choice of every cuisine.

Here are some suggestions:

Czech cuisine

U Čížků, Karlovo nám. 34, Nové Město.
One of the most pleasant restaurants in Prague.
Bohemia, Václavské nám. 29, Nové Město.
Best to go when you're really starving, because this place offers a huge buffet style Czech feast.
Pod křídlem, Voršilská Street, Nové Město.
The location of this modern but very romantic place is ideal for visitors to National Theatre or Laterna Magica.
Mucha, Melantrichova 5, Staré Město.
A restaurant in art-nouveau style, dedicated to painter Alfons Mucha. Highly recommended for the Old Town Square area.
Česká hospoda, Krakovská St.
A typical Czech pub with delicious food.
U Sixtů, Celetná 2, Staré Město.
In a Gothic cellar with superb atmosphere.
Pezinok, Purkyňova 4.
Slovak-style restaurant with the essential Gypsy band.
U červeného kola, Anežská 2, Staré Město.
Warm and pleasant atmosphere to make a wonderful evening.
U staré synagogy, Pařížská 17, Staré Město.
Jewish restaurant in the heart of the former ghetto district.
Vikárka, Vikářská 4, Hradčany.
Restaurant with long tradition, just behind St. Vitus Cathedral in the Prague Castle area.
Parnas, Smetanovo nábř. 2.
Offers a splendid view of Prague Castle and Charles Bridge.
U zlaté hrušky, Nový svět 3, Hradčany.
In one of the most superb settings in Prague, where they re-invent old Bohemian rhapsodies.

Restaurants with a view

Bohemia, at TV Tower Praha.
Very good food and a fantastic view, from a height of 63 metres.

Nebozízek, Petřínské Hill, at first stop on the funicular railway. Try to be seated on the outdoor terrace, overlooking one of Prague's most romantic spots.

Vegetarian restaurants

Góvinda – Vegetarian club of Hare Kršna, Na hrázi 5, Prague 8.
Delikates Bar, Palace Hotel, Jindřišská St., Nové Město.
Country life, Vodičková St., Nové Město.
Gafrijjola (Fruit shop), Budečská 35, Prague 2.
FX Café (above the Radost Club), Bělehradská 120, Prague 2.

Fish restaurants

Rybárna, Václavské náměstí 43, Nové Město
  Fish specialities, particularly carp.
Na rybárně, Gorazdova 7, Prague 2.
  Price range modest.
U modré štiky, Karlova St.
  Prices about average.
U Vojáčků, Vodní 11, Prague 5.
  Price range modest.

Cafés

Amadeus / Kamenný stůl, Old Town Square 18.
  Café on the first floor of historical building offering delicious sweets and wide range of coffees.
Café bar U Minuty, Old Town Square 3.
  In the house where Franz Kafka lived, one of the best cafés in town.
Columbia café, Mostecká 3.
  Genuine Columbian coffee and original liqueurs and cognacs, plus great sweets.
Rock café, Národní třída 20.
  Bar featuring rock and hard-rock, with well-known Czech and foreign groups.
Metropolitan Club, Jungmannova 14.
  Drinks and cold dishes with live swing, blues, ragtime and jazz.
Café Evropa, Václavské nám. 25.
  Situated in one of Prague's most impressive hotels.
Slavia, Národní třída 1
  Facing National Theatre, a traditional café restored to its former elegance.

Beer Taverns

The Czech Republic is understandably famed for its beer, rated as the world's best. Here are some recommended ale-houses in central Prague. Mostly they also serve meals or very substantial snacks at modest prices.
U Fleků, Křemencova 11, Nové Město
  (At the Fleks). Sells bitter-brewed only, Flek dark 13° beer. Dating from 1459, it is Prague's oldest beer house.

U kalicha, Na bojišti 12, Nové Město
(The Chalice). Excellent food, good bar. Former haunt of the author of *Good Soldier Schweik* – a satire on war and bureaucracy. This was Schweik's favourite bar.

U supa, Celetná 22, Staré Město
One of the best-known Prague taverns. The speciality is Bráník beer.

Hospoda U dvou koček, Uhelný trh 10, Staré Město
(The Two Cats). Lovely little tavern with real Prague atmosphere, and selling Pilsner Urquell 12° beer. Friendly staff with excellent service and food.

U Svatého Tomáše, Letenská 12, Malá Strana
(At St. Thomas's). One of the oldest brewers, founded in 1352. Sells very good Bráník dark 12° beer.

U zlatého tygra, Husova 17
The Golden Tiger serves Pilsner.

Baráčnická rychta, Nerudova 13.

Wine bars and cellars

Most of the wines comes from Bulgaria, Romania or Hungary.

U pastýřky, Bělehradská 12.
Lobkovická vinárna, Vlašská 17.
Slovácká vícha, Michalská 6.
U zelené žáby, U radnice 8.
U plebána, Betlémské nám. 10.
U tří housliček, Nerudova 12.
Blatnice, Michalská 6.

4.10 Nightlife

Something for your first evening, to give a dazzling first impression of the Czech capital: find your way to the Old Town Hall Square. After-dark illuminations highlight the pastel colours with gorgeous clarity. Then stroll to Charles Bridge, which offers a superb view across the River Vltava to the brilliantly lit Jesuit church of St. Nicholas Church and thence to the skyline towers of Prague Castle. The bridge itself is thronged with sightseers and entertainers.

Otherwise, much of Prague's nightlife focusses around a leisured dinner in a traditional restaurant, or among the beer-halls and wine taverns.

On the cultural circuit, Prague has an excellent ballet company at the National Theatre and has three opera houses and five symphony orchestras. Evening programmes at theatres and concerts usually begin at 19.00 or 19.30 hrs. Dress is formal. If you like music, try to schedule your trip for the Prague Spring Festival in May.

The **Laterna Magika** offers a unique theatrical experience – a remarkable mixture of dance, film, theatre and dramatic lighting effects. Try your utmost to get tickets!

4.11   At your service

Money and Banking

The currency unit in the Czech Republic is the koruna (Crown), abbreviated Kč. There are 100 hellers in a Czech Crown. Since the partition of Czechoslovakia, the former currency has been replaced by separate Czech and Slovak Crowns. Be sure that your banknotes read 'Korun Českých'.

Coins are of 10, 20 and 50 hellers; and 1, 2, 5, 10, 20 and 50 Kčs. Notes are of 20, 50, 100, 200, 500, 1000, 2000 and 5000 crowns.

Changing money

You can change at the airport, in your hotel, at a bank or at the numerous exchange bureaux in tourist locations. Commission rates are widely spread, and it pays to shop around before changing larger amounts. The handy city-centre exchange kiosks are particularly heavy on commission. But try the exchange office on Vodičkova Street, opposite McDonald's. Otherwise, two recommendations:

Thomas Cook on Narodni Street; and at the Motokov (close to Panorama Hotel). Open Mon-Fri 9-20 hrs; Sat 9-16 hrs; Sun 10-14 hrs.

American Express at 56 Wenceslas Square. Open Mon-Fri 9-18 hrs; Sat 9-12 hrs. Best rates for AMEX traveller cheques; not so good for changing cash.

You can exchange cash without producing your passport, but it's needed when changing traveller cheques. Keep your exchange dockets, so you can readily re-convert any surplus on departure. The main international credit cards are accepted in the principal hotels, restaurants and shops that display the credit card symbol.

In contrast to former years when there was a big gap between official and black market rates, the exchange rate is 'realistic' and favourable. The Czech crown holds remarkably firm against Western currencies. Unofficial street deals that offer a 'better' rate are not worth the risk of light-fingered switching.

Which toilet door?

Toilets are marked WC or 00. Women's are labelled 'Dámy' or 'Ženy'. Men's are 'Páni' or 'Muži'.

Public holidays

January 1	New Year's Day
May 1	May Day
May 8	Liberation Day
July 5 & 6	State holidays
October 28	Independence Day
December 24, 25, 26	Christmas

Easter Monday is also a public holiday.

Useful Addresses and Phone Numbers

Lost Property
Karoliny Suetle 5, Prague 1   Tel: 24235085

Embassies
Great Britain, Thunovská 1, Malá Strana
                                               Tel: 57320355
USA, Tržiště 15, Malá Strana   Tel: 57320663

Medical
If you see a doctor while in Prague and have to pay for the consultation, obtain a receipt both from the doctor and the chemist. This is required for claiming refund under the terms of any insurance you have. In general, medical attention is provided free of charge for British subjects.

Chemist: Charles Sq or Wenceslas Sq   Tel: 24210229
First Aid: Tel: 517111

Post Office and Telephone
General Post Office, Jindřišká 14   Tel: 24228856
Prague Central Station (open 24 hours)   Tel: 24224200
International calls: see dialling notes in chapter 1.3. For English-speaking international operator, dial 0132.

Tourist Information
Čedok, Na příkopě 18
Information Centre, Hradčanská Metro
Prague Information Service, Na příkopě 2Tel: 24197642
Cityrama   Tel: 24911122

Emergency Telephone Numbers
First Aid   155
Ambulance   373333
Dentist   261374
Police   158
Fire   150

Newspapers
In central Prague the earliest English-language papers to arrive are *The Guardian*, *Financial Times*, *International Herald Tribune* and *The Wall Street Journal* – all printed on the Continent. Other London newspapers and magazines arrive later. For local background, read the weekly *Prague Post*, which also lists Coming Events.

Chapter Five

Budapest

5.1 Introduction to Budapest

For the best panorama of Budapest, stand on Gellért Hill – a rock that rises steeply, 430 feet above the river bank. Below is the Danube, an average 450 yards wide. The river cuts the Hungarian capital into two: the hills of Buda on the right bank; the plain of Pest on the left.

The Buda hills formed the original settlement: Castle Hill, with a fortress and Royal Palace, the ancient Matthias Church where Hungarian kings were crowned for 600 years, and the more modern Fishermen's Bastion which is another fine viewing point. *See map fig. 7.*

All around on Castle Hill are delightful old streets of medieval, baroque and classical houses. This is the romantic old-time Budapest that flourished when Budapest was part of the Austro-Hungarian Empire.

Across the Danube bridges lies the Inner City, called Belváros – the heart of old Pest, which originally was independent of Buda. Within that Inner City it's mainly an 18th- and 19th-century world of baroque churches, turn-of-the-century shops, cafés and restaurants, and a ministerial and political nucleus that focusses around the neo-gothic Parliament House that looks like a riverside copy of London's Parliament without Big Ben.

Further up-stream, the River Danube splits into two arms that form Margaret Island – 200 acres of public park used as a major sport and recreation centre. Like a complete resort, it has tennis courts, swimming pools with artificial waves, amusement centres, rose-gardens, open-air theatres, cafés, restaurants and a Grand Hotel.

And all around is the Danube, with paddle-steamers, hydrofoils and launches that offer a variety of river trips, some with meals, music and dancing.

On Margaret Island you can sample a bathing-pool of hot sulphur water, fed by one of Budapest's 123 thermal springs – a big share of the 400 mineral springs that exist in Hungary as a whole. The Romans fell in love with Budapest because of the hot baths, and visitors have been taking the waters ever since. At the bottom of Gellért Hill is a large spa hotel with all hot-spring amenities.

The break from Moscow

Budapest ranks as Eastern Europe's liveliest capital, having made an early break from the heavy Moscow style. The process accelerated, with dumping of red stars, much faster moves towards a market economy, opening of a Stock Exchange, and renaming of streets that had been dedicated to the former ideology. The renaming process has now been completed, and most city maps have been updated.

Budapest is a musical city. Gipsy bands are everywhere: in hotels at teatime, to accompany coffee and cake; in speciality restaurants; in wine-cellars that stay open till past midnight; on Danube steamers that offer evening cruises.

Often the musicians are dressed in formal evening suits with black bow-ties; otherwise they are brightly clad in traditional costume, all ready to smile at the flashguns. Their gipsy music is enchanting, switching from mood to mood through an evening of Magyar nostalgia.

On a more serious note, Budapest can offer the widest possible choice of classical music, year-round.

In summer the main attraction of Budapest is sightseeing: the scenery, the Danube and excursions to Lake Balaton. In winter, visitors come especially for the mental refreshment of cultural events, with the added attraction that off-season hotel prices are much lower. But always there's great pleasure in sampling the rich variety of Hungarian cuisine, supported by the excellent Hungarian wines. A few days in Budapest can be a very memorable experience.

5.2 Arrival & hotel

No visas are required for UK passport holders. By air, London Heathrow to Budapest is served daily by either British Airways or Malév. There are daily flights from Vienna by Malév or Austrian Airlines. By train from Vienna's Westbahnhof takes about 5 hours.

Two public buses operate daily from Vienna to Budapest, taking 4½ hours. A more expensive alternative is to cruise along the Danube by hydrofoil, to disembark by Elizabeth Bridge (Erzsébet hid).

If you're arriving by air, transfer to your hotel is by bus or taxi, taking about 30 minutes to the centre. The best transport deal is by Airport Minibus to any city destination for Ft. 1200 (about £4). Book tickets in the baggage arrival hall, and go to the meeting point in the main hall.

Hotels follow the international grading system of one to five stars. Most of them are very central, mainly on the Pest side of the river within walking distance of the main sights or easily reached in a few minutes by the very frequent and low-cost public transport.

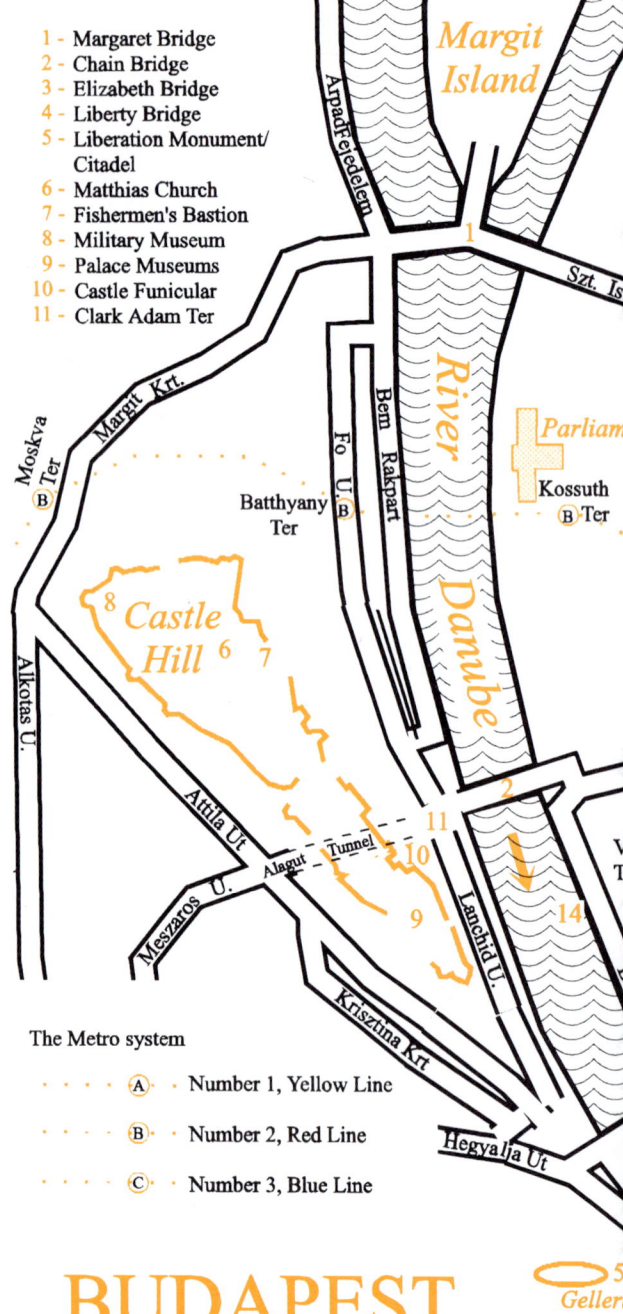

1 - Margaret Bridge
2 - Chain Bridge
3 - Elizabeth Bridge
4 - Liberty Bridge
5 - Liberation Monument/
    Citadel
6 - Matthias Church
7 - Fishermen's Bastion
8 - Military Museum
9 - Palace Museums
10 - Castle Funicular
11 - Clark Adam Ter

The Metro system

· · · · Ⓐ · Number 1, Yellow Line

· · · · Ⓑ · Number 2, Red Line

· · · · Ⓒ · Number 3, Blue Line

BUDAPEST

N

20

17 18
19
Hosok
Tere

Bajza Utca

Kodaly-Korond

Nyugati
Ter

Terez Krt.

Vorosmarty
Utca

Octagon

Andrassy Ut

16

Erzsebet Krt.

Bajcsy-Zsilinszky Ut

Arany
Janos U

15

Opera

Bajcsy-
Zsilinszky Ut

Deak
Ter.

marty

Karoly Krt.

Rakoczi Ut

Blaha
Lujza
Ter

Jozsef Krt.

Vaci Utca

Astoria

Kossuth U.

Muzeum Krt.

Felsz-
abadulas
Ter

13

Kalvin Ter

Baross U.

Vaci Utca

Vamhaz Krt.

Ulloi U.

Ferenc
Korut

12

4

Raknart

Gellert

0   200   400

metres

5.3 *Getting around Budapest*

Public transport offers you wide choice of trams, trolley buses, buses and Metro. There are no conductors. Following the usual Central European honour system, passengers punch their own ticket when they board. Tickets and day passes can be bought at tobacco shops, tram and bus terminals, railway stations, and at travel offices.

These tickets are valid for use any distance on buses, trams, trolley buses, Metro and the suburban railway (HÉV) as far as the city limits.

The most convenient Best Buy is the 3-day Budapest Card costing about £8 or £10, giving unlimited public transport, free entry to 55 museums and many shopping and dining discounts.

Trams
There are 38 tram routes on a very frequent schedule from 4 a.m. till midnight. A few main lines operate all night. A very useful service is 2 and 2A, which shuttles along the Pest river embankment.

Buses
The blue Ikarus buses operate on 208 bus routes. Buses with black numbers stop at every halt on their route.

Those with red numbers are express services stopping only at specially indicated halts.

Those with letter E after a red number travel non-stop from one terminal to another. Services operate 04.30 till 23.00 hrs, with a few main routes operating all night.

Metro
There are three Metro lines – easy to use, and all meeting at Deák tér. They operate between 4.30 a.m. and 23.10 hrs (till midnight on yellow line).

Number 1, yellow line, runs between Mexikói út and Vörösmarty tér.

Number 2, red line, operates between Őrs Vezér tere and the Déli Pályaudvar (Southern Railway Sation).

Number 3, blue line, runs between Kőbánya-Kispest MÁV Állomás (railway station) and Ujpest Város Központ.

The most useful stations for visitors are:

Vörösmarty tér for the heart of the pedestrianized shopping streets along Váci utca; also closest to the three riverside luxury hotels – Atrium Hyatt, Inter-Continental and Marriott. **Deák tér** is also very close.

Kossuth tér is nearest to the Parliament building.

Astoria or **Kálvin tér** are handy for National Museum.

Hősök tere (Heroes' Square) is best for the Fine Art Museum and for the Agricultural Museum in Vajdahunyad Castle and Városliget Park.

From **Moszkva tér**, a little blue bus labelled Budavári Sikló takes you quickly up the steep hill to the Castle area, with several stops inside the ramparts.

Funicular
A very useful funicular operates from Buda side of the Chain Bridge up to the Royal Palace in Castle District, with splendid views by day or night.

Trolley buses
Twelve trolley routes, mostly connecting with the Metro.

HÉV (Suburban Railway)
This service offers connections to villages surrounding the capital. There are four lines: Gödöllő, Csepel, Ráckeve and Szentendre. The Szentendre line is particularly important, serving that beautiful resort village on the Danube (see section 5.6). Its starting point is Batthyány tér on Metro red line.

Other transport services include a cogwheel railway, river boats and minibuses.

Taxis
You can order by calling Főtaxi 222-2222 or Volántaxi 352-8953. To reserve a taxi in advance dial 118-8888.

Cabs are metered in the usual way, but Western vehicles like Mercedes are more expensive than those from Eastern Europe. Generally, if you're watching your funds, don't catch a taxi outside the big hotels. The fare could easily double. Tipping: for short distances, make it 15%; otherwise 10%.

Sightseeing coaches
A favourite style of Budapest sightseeing is by coach tour with a high-grade city guide. Excellent excursions are operated by Cityrama Budapest, which is linked to the international Gray Line organisation. Office address is Báthori utca 22. Tel: 3325344; Fax: 3125424.

Orientation
Four main bridges link the sightseeing zones of Buda and Pest.
Margaret Bridge – Margit hid – gives access to the mid-Danube park of Margaret Island. *See map fig. 1.*

91

BUDAPEST

Chain Bridge – Széchenyi Lánchid. From Roosevelt Square beside the Atrium Hyatt hotel you can cross to Buda on the Chain Bridge which was built by a British engineer, Adam Clark, in the 1840's. *Map fig. 2.* It was the first bridge across the Danube at this point. From Clark Ádám Square a major road – also built by Adam Clark – tunnels below Castle Hill, while the funicular offers an easy ride to the summit. A circular stone carving near the funicular marks the zero point from which all Hungarian distances from Budapest are measured.

Elizabeth Bridge – Erzsébet hid – is named after Emperor Franz Joseph's wife who was assassinated in 1898. An original chain bridge was demolished by the Germans in 1945, and replaced by a suspension bridge in 1964. *See map fig. 3.*

Liberty Bridge – Szabadság hid – leads from the Central Market area (see section 5.8) to Gellért Hill. *Fig. 4.*

River Port

On the Pest side, between Elizabeth and Liberty Bridge, the river bank serves as an international river port and frontier zone! This is where passport formalities are conducted for passengers aboard international boats such as the hydrofoil service from Vienna.

5.4 Basic Budapest

Here's a short list of Essential Budapest, aimed at capturing the flavour of this lively capital.

(1) Make the most of the standard City Sightseeing tour, which includes time at magnificent viewpoints like Gellért Hill and the Fishermen's Bastion. *See map figs. 5 & 7.*

(2) Spend several hours, daytime or evening, exploring the streets and buildings of Castle Hill.

(3) Take an evening dinner cruise on the Danube with gipsy music and wild Hungarian folk-dancing.

(4) Sample rich pastries at Gerbaud's on Vörösmarty Square.

(5) Shop-gaze along Váci utca, and look for bargains in folk art, books, records, Herend porcelain and Helia-D cosmetics.

(6) See the Hungarian crown jewels on first floor of the National Museum. *See map fig. 13.*

(7) Enjoy an evening stroll along the Dunakorzó Promenade, now lined with big international hotels.

(8) Travel to the beautiful Danube Bend by coach or boat, with time to explore Szentendre.

(9) Wallow in the thermal baths at Hotel Gellért or at Thermal on Margit Island, as reminder of why Roman soldiers enjoyed a posting to this city.

(10) Visit the Central Market Hall (*map fig. 12*), near Szabadság Bridge for colourful displays of farm products.

A guided sightseeing tour of Budapest is the best introduction to the city. If you haven't already booked, contact your rep for a reservation. The Cityrama Grand City Tour takes three hours, and includes pickup from your hotel before the scheduled departure time.

The two halves of Budapest couldn't be more different. On one side of the Danube ancient Buda rises and falls over seven hills. On the other side, Pest – the government and commercial centre of the capital – is impressive with its grand boulevards, squares and buildings.

The Castle District of Buda

Most visitors return several times to Castle Hill, which offers fascination at every turn: cobbled streets, Baroque mansions and medieval courtyards high above the rest of the city. The entire district was devastated when German Nazi troops held out against the Russian army from December 1944 until mid-February 1945. It took 20 years to complete the restoration, totally in the original harmonious style.

Matthias Church – Mátyás templom. *See map fig. 6.*
The Church of Our Lady with its slender Gothic spire is also known as the Coronation church, where a number of Hungarian kings were crowned. More often it's called Matthias Church, after the 15th-century King Matthias whose coat of arms appears on the south tower.

During Turkish occupation, the building was converted into the city's principal mosque. After the return of Christian forces, it was then rebuilt in Baroque style, followed in the 19th century by yet another reconstruction in neo-Gothic. Within, the cathedral still shows some stylized Islamic decoration – on the columns, for instance – as reminder of the building's 150 years as a mosque.

The church stands on Holy Trinity Square – named after the 18th-century Trinity Statue erected in thanksgiving for deliverance from the plague. The square is focalpoint for private-sector tourism. Here is pick-up point for horse-and-buggy rides. The drivers charge 600 to 1000 Ft for a 15-minute trot around. Buskers and handicraft vendors spill over into the Fishermen's Bastion area, which is thick with instant-portrait artists and currency hustlers.

Fishermen's Bastion – Halász Bástya. *See map fig. 7.*
Although this monument could pass as medieval with its turrets, terraces and arches it was actually built early this century. According to tradition this stretch of the medieval ramparts was defended by the fishermen's guild, hence the name. The panorama is magnificent, across the Danube to the Parliament building and right round to Gellért Hill.

93

Alongside is the Budapest Hilton, which – despite its ultra-modern appearance with copper-glass facade – fits in quite well, and doesn't spoil the view from across the river. Three parallel side streets lead off from Holy Trinity Square (Szentháromság tér) and Hess András tér – Táncsics Mihály utca, Fortuna utca and Országház utca. Virtually every other building displays a plaque marking it as a historic monument. The beautiful baroque houses and mansions all have medieval foundations. You can easily cover the area in a one-hour stroll. But it's worth spending longer to absorb the atmosphere, perhaps staying for an evening meal and seeing the area under the added glamour of nightfall. Look specially for these highlights:

Táncsics Mihály utca – In medieval times, this was a Jewish street – no. 26 is the Jewish Oratory with relics excavated from that time. The street is named after the revolutionary writer who was imprisoned at no. 9 with Lajos Kossuth in 1848. Previously that building housed the Royal Mint. Next door, no. 7, was formerly the Erdődy Palace where Beethoven stayed in 1800. It's now the **Museum of Music History**, with musical instruments displayed in the workshop of Béla Bartók. (Open Wed-Sun 10-18 hrs; Mon 16-21 hrs; closed Tue.)

Fortuna utca – At no. 4 is the **Museum of Commerce and Catering** which displays everything from old menus to kitchen utensils and the confectionery business. The commerce section covers history of trade in the first half of the 20th century. The building itself was previously the Fortuna Inn.

Országház utca (Parliament Street) – Look particularly at nos. 18, 20 and 22, which were built in 14th and 15th centuries and give an idea of how the Castle District looked in medieval times. During Turkish occupation, several baths – hamams – were located along this street.

At the far end of these three streets is the Esztergom Bastion which completes the castle ramparts, with an exit called Vienna Gate – walk up for yet another viewpoint. The **Museum of Military History** on Tóth Árpád Promenade covers the history of hand weapons, knights from the time of King Matthias, the Revolution and War of Independence of 1848-49; World War 1, and the Hungarian army from 1920 to the present. (Open: daily except Mon, 9-18 hrs.) *See map fig. 8.*

Back to Trinity Square, Tárnok utca or Uri utca both lead towards the upper end of the cable car from Chain Bridge, and to the Royal Palace. Along those two streets are some more beautifully reconstructed houses. Several embassies are located in this area. At Uri utca 9 is entry to some damp Catacombs.

Buda Castle Palace – *See map fig. 9.*

The Palace you see today originally developed from a modest 13th century construction. As different monarchs came to power each wanted to impress their countrymen with an even more splendid Palace. The neo-Baroque building today evolved during reconstruction in the 19th and 20th centuries. It has been completely rebuilt since the siege of 1945 when it was used by the Germans as a command post. From the parapet you can see how the palace-castle totally dominated the river crossing.

As the largest public building in Budapest, the Palace now houses three museums – National Gallery, Budapest History Museum and the National Library. The **National Gallery** has the most interest for visitors, featuring Hungarian art from 14th century onwards, but specially rich in evocative late 19th-century painting.

At the front entrance to the Royal Palace, overlooking the Danube, is a statue of Prince Eugene of Savoy, the Austrian general who ejected the Turks from their 150 years' occupation of the city.

Gellért Hill – *See map fig. 5.*

Another style of Liberation Monument rears dramatically 45 feet high on top of Gellért Hill, and is visible from all parts of the city. A statue of a woman holding a palm leaf of freedom is symbolic of liberation from Nazi rule, and was erected in 1947. Behind the monument is the Citadel – a fortress built in mid-19th century by the Austrians, after the collapse of the Hungarian War of Independence. Within the once-menacing walls are a restaurant, café and hotel.

Gellért Hill is named after the Italian missionary Bishop Ghirardus (Gellért), who converted the country to Christianity. He died a martyr's death in 1046, when pagan Hungarians nailed him into a barrel and rolled him off the clifftop. His personal monument faces Elizabeth Bridge, along the steep route down to the river.

Rudas Baths (Rudas fürdű)

At the bottom of Gellért Hill, close to Elizabeth Bridge, are the men-only Rudas thermal baths, built by the Turks in 1556. Although the building has been altered substantially over the years a splendid Turkish dome still rises over one octagonal pool. When the sun shines through, it creates dramatic effects.

By Szabadság Bridge is the famous Gellért Hotel and Baths, built 1913 to offer spa treatment.

Belváros – the Inner City

During medieval times, while Buda's Castle Hill was settled by people dependent on the palaces and forts, the east bank was the tradesmen's end: a quite separate town called Pest (pronounced 'Pesht'). A city wall marked the boundary, which is followed today by the so-called Kiskörút (Little Boulevard) – from Liberty Bridge to Chain Bridge via Múzeum körút, Károly körút, József Attila utca and Roosevelt Square – with the curving river bank to form a lemon-shaped area of tightly-packed 19th-century building.

Vörösmarty tér and Váci utca

One of Pest's main centres is the square called Vörösmarty tér, named after a 19th-century patriotic poet whose statue stands in the middle. In summertime dozens of artists offer an on-the-spot portrait service, with entertainers to supply background music.

This square leads into the cosmopolitan **Váci utca**, which runs parallel to the Danube, behind the big international hotels. Together with the side streets, and up to Deák Square, it all makes a very pleasant pedestrian precinct. Day and night it's a lively area, with some of the best shops, boutiques, cafés amd restaurants of Budapest. Special for capitalists who want to buy bonds: the former Eastern bloc's first Stock Exchange opened on Váci Street in 1990.

Dunakorzó – the Danube Promenade

Stroll along the Danube waterfront for the glorious panorama of the Buda Hills across the river. Three large international hotels – Atrium Hyatt, Inter-Continental and Marriott – have given a new postwar look to the promenade, which was a prewar favourite for a leisured stroll.

Vigadó Square is embarcation point for pleasure cruises – a wide range of choices, some with meals and music. The square takes its name from the Vigadó Concert Hall dating from 1865. Besides its large concert hall, the building includes a small theatre, restaurant and a magnificent staircase. *See map fig. 14.*

Parliament – Országház

Facing the Chain Bridge is Roosevelt Square. Continue further along the embankment to reach Kossuth Lajos Square and the Parliament building.

In a mixture of Renaissance and Gothic, the building was originally constructed to reflect the grandeur of the Austro-Hungarian Empire. In style and riverside location it greatly resembles London's Houses of Parliament.

Facing Parliament is the Ministry of Agriculture and then another look-alike: the **Ethnographic Museum**, which could double for the Berlin Reichstag.

This neo-Renaissance palace was built in the 1890's and now houses collections from ancient times to modern days.

On the square between these buildings is a statue of Kossuth Lajos, who was a leader of the Hungarian Independence movement of 1848. Crucial political demonstrations have swirled around his statue.

Elsewhere on the square – among trees by the embankment – is a dreamy statue of Attila József, a poet who lived 1905 to 1937. Especially he is known for his poem about sitting beside the river, just watching the water float by. Maybe that's an even better way of enjoying Basic Budapest.

5.5 Other sights in Budapest

Museums and art galleries

Unless otherwise noted, museums are open daily except Mondays from 10-18 or 9-17 hrs. Entrance prices are minimal.

National Museum, Múzeum körút 14-16. *Map fig. 13.*

Looking like a smaller version of the British Museum, this is Hungary's most important collection, and includes history of the Hungarian peoples. Among the Coronation Regalia is the crown of St. Stephen which spent over 30 years in USA, until its return in 1978.

Museum of Fine Arts, Dózsa György út 41, Hősök tere – Heroes' Square. *See map fig. 17.*

Displays the Egyptian collection, a rich supply of old masters, graphic arts, and modern painting and sculpture. For art lovers, this museum rates very high among Europe's galleries – far richer than most people expect. The collection of Spanish paintings is outstanding.

Museum of Applied Art, IX, Üllői út 33-37

Varied art and crafts; and tapestries from late 19th century till World War 11. The collection is especially rich in Art Nouveau or Secessionist style – worth seeing for this alone.

Aquincum Museum, III, Szentendrei út 139

Remains of the Roman city, along the road towards Szentendre. Open May to October.

Transport Museum, XIV, Városligeti körút 11

In Városliget Park – numerous displays, with working models.

Andrássy ut

This grand boulevard has reverted to its former name, after years of being called Népköztársaság utja – Avenue of the People's Republic – and still shown thus, on some city maps.

Its style resembles the Champs Elysées in Paris, ending in Heroes' Square for the big State occasions. It reaches from the Inner Boulevard to the City park. Most of the buildings date from between 1872 and 1885, and have some unique feature such as a fountain or statue in their courtyards.

Bus 4 runs the whole distance, while underground is the century-old Metro line 1 – the oldest in continental Europe. Train buffs should visit the Metro Museum in the Deák Square pedestrian underpass – open Wed-Sun. The main buildings along the avenue include:

Postal Museum at no. 3 – Relics from Post Office history, telecommunications, and 60 years of radio.

State Opera House at no. 22, restored to its original splendour. *See map fig. 15.* The associated **Operett Theatre** – mainly playing operettas – is located in Nagymező utca. **Ballet Institute** at no. 25.

Hungarian Academy of Music in a square (right) called Liszt Ferenc tér with a statue of Franz Liszt in the middle. The Academy, built 1904-07 in Art Nouveau style, houses a large concert hall. *See map fig. 16.*

Ferenc Liszt Museum at no. 67, the composer's former home. (Open Mon-Fri 10-18 hrs; Sat 9-17 hrs.)

Academy of Fine Arts at no. 71. *See map fig. 16.*

Composer **Zoltán Kodály**'s former residence at no. 89.

Heroes' Square – Hősök tere

The 47-ton centrepiece to Heroes' Square is the Millenary Monument erected in 1896 to commemorate the 1,000th anniversary of Magyar conquest of the country. There are statues of leading figures in Hungarian history – kings, tribal chiefs and war heroes. Easiest access is direct by Metro line 1 from downtown.

The Museum of Fine Arts (see above) and an Art Gallery Exhibition Hall (looking like a Greek temple) are located each side of the square, with Városliget – City Park – in the background.

Until 1956, postwar visitors viewed a huge statue of **Stalin** on a vast plinth behind the Exhibition Hall (Mücsarnok). But he was chopped up during the opening hours of the Hungarian Revolution in October 1956. He was replaced by Lenin, who has likewise since been removed. The plinth is still there.

Városliget – City Park

Right behind Heroes' Square is Budapest's largest park – 250 green acres that include a boating lake which becomes an ice rink in winter. Across the lake, reflected in the waters, is the make-believe **Castle of Vajdahunyad**. *See map fig. 19.* Like the monument in Heroes' Square, it was built as part of the millenary celebrations of 1896. The aim was to incorporate every architectural style used in Hungary's 1,000-year history.

The building houses an **Agricultural Museum** which covers farming, fishing and hunting. (Open daily except Mon 10-16 hrs.) In the courtyard is a mysterious hooded statue of Anonymous, the unknown Royal Scribe who wrote the first Hungarian chronicles.

The park also houses the triple domed **Széchenyi**

Baths – one of Europe's largest medicinal bath complexes – as well as Gundel's luxury-grade restaurant, the giant beer tent of the Royal Bavarian Brewery, a small zoo and botanical garden, an amusement park for the kids, and the Transport Museum. Altogether it's a good place to see how Hungarians relax.

Margaret Island – Margitsziget

This Danube island is about 1.5 miles long, virtually traffic free and protected from noise by planted plane-trees.

It's a favourite spot for a peaceful two-hour stroll. Among the attractions are swimming complexes, an open-air theatre, open-air cinema, and a thermal water spring with goldfish. Enjoy the tranquil terrace setting of the Ramada Grand Hotel.

Buda Hills

As a change from city sightseeing take the cog wheel train to Liberty Hill. The terminal is opposite Hotel Budapest on Szilágyi Erzsébet fasor – access from Moszkva tér on tram no. 18 or 56.

You travel through greenery, villas and gardens into open spaces where, close to the last stop, you can ride on the **Pioneer Railway**. This is operated by school children dressed in the smart uniforms of station masters, ticket sellers and conductors.

Summer visitors can take the chair-lift (Libegő) to the top of János Hill where it is possible to see more than 45 miles on a clear day. There's access from Moszkva tér on bus no. 158.

5.6 Take a trip

Danube Bend

The prime excursion out of Budapest is upstream to the Danube Bend, where the river narrows and turns sharply as it passes between the 2500-3000 ft heights of the Pilis and the Börzsöny Mountains.

The strategic Bend is overlooked by the hilltop fortress palace of **Visegrád** – first developed by the Romans, then built up by the Hungarian kings from 13th century onwards. This was the official royal seat in the early Middle Ages – not in Buda. By the 15th century, Visegrád rated high among the great palaces of Central Europe.

Destroyed by the Turks in 1542, the site was forgotten until rediscovered in 1934.

Since then, restoration has given Visegrád very high rating as a tourist attraction. There are superb views of the Danube Bend itself, and of controversial preparations for a mammoth hydro-electric complex – now abandoned through popular outcry.

Szentendre

En route to Visegrád is Szentendre – a small and charming riverside town which originally was settled by Greek and Serbian migrants. Szentendre has become a mini resort, with numerous cafés, restaurants and cheerful souvenir shops, boutiques and peasant craftware stalls.

Open-air museum

Near Szentendre is the Skanzen: a museum of peasant houses and village buildings which have been transported from different parts of Hungary, re-erected and furnished in authentic style. On certain days young people perform traditional activities, like harvesting and making bread.

Danube Bend excursions are operated by motor coach or river boat. Part of the pleasure comes from admiring the prosperous-looking private homes along the road, each standing in its own large garden, packed with flowers, fruit and vegetables. Many houses offer rooms to let – "Zimmer frei"

Lake Balaton

A popular arrangement is to split summer holiday time between Budapest and Lake Balaton. The 48-mile lake is the largest inland sea of Central Europe, and is well developed for the sunshine business.

A splendid landmark is the twin-spired abbey church dominating the Tihany peninsula that almost cuts the lake in half.

The lake shores are shallow and offer warm bathing. There are beaches, little yacht harbours, and facilities for water sports and fishing.

But the greatest delight comes from exploring the wine villages, and tasting the vintages. There are photo possibilities everywhere you look. Long single-storeyed farmhouses are thatched and lime-washed.

If you can spare another day from your Budapest City Break, put Balaton high on your list of where to go!

5.7 Sunday in Budapest

All shops are closed, but cafés, restaurants, museums, art galleries and sightseeing tours are in full operation.

For High Mass in a superb setting, go to Matthias Church in the Castle District. *See map fig. 6.* An orchestra and choir perform classical sacred works every Sunday at 10 a.m.

Inner City Parish Church – Belvárosi Templom

This is the oldest surviving structure in Pest, located on the approach to Elizabeth Bridge. The twin Baroque towers and the facade date from early 19th Century, but the church was founded in 12th Century.

Basilica (St Stephen's Parish Church)

This is the biggest church in Budapest and took from 1851 to 1905 to complete. The church holds 8,000 people, and is often filled to capacity during services.

Sunday Markets

XI Fehérvári út 14. (6-13 hrs)
XIII Lehel tér. (6-14 hrs)

5.8 Shopping in Budapest

What to buy?

Food and Drink: browse through the supermarkets for Hungarian salami, paprika spice, golden Tokaj and a bottle of barack apricot brandy. Maybe you have acquired a taste for all four, so what better memento, along with a few bottles of Bull's Blood?

Handicrafts: survey the folk-art shops for hand-woven cushion covers, costume dolls, lace and embroidered tablecloths which mostly come from Transylvania. Copper and brass bowls, vases, ashtrays etc make good presents. Look for leather goods, silver, woodwork and precious stones. Carpets and rugs are reasonably priced, even those which are homespun and hand-knotted.

Ceramics: the most famous factory, at Herend near Veszprém north of Lake Balaton, has been producing porcelain since 1839. Queen Victoria ordered some for Windsor Castle in 1851, and the White House bought Herend ware for state banquets. The hand-painted designs are in rich variety, 19th-century rather than modern: animal pieces galore, floral patterns and Ming-like teapots and pedestal cake stands. Figurines of typical Hungarian characters are also popular.

Books, records and games: there are some excellent books in English, remarkably low-cost. Also worth buying are recordings of Hungarian folk-music, classical CD's and cassettes; and teasers in three-dimensional logic – successors to the Rubik Cube – from the Rubik Studio.

Hair tonic: finally, a curiosity – many visitors buy bottles of a famous tonic and cure-all called Béres Csepp. This and Bánfi hair lotion for thinning hair – said to halt the process – can be found in Herbaria shops.

Shopping areas

The principal shops are along the Great Boulevard formed by the boulevards of Szt István, Teréz, József and Ferenc; and along Kossuth Lajos Street which continues as Rákóczi út. These streets are lined with shops and department stores with a broad range of goods.

More fun for most visitors is the pedestrian precinct with up-market fashion shops and coffee bars centring on

Váci Street from Vörösmarty Square to Kígyó Street and Petőfi Sándor Street. This area is Budapest's Bond Street. It's also a pleasant place for an evening stroll, when the shops are closed but you can still window-gaze at the lively displays.

Across the river in the Castle District, high-quality boutiques and folk-art shops are geared to tourism, and charge ambitious prices. There is wide range of fashion accessories. Look, for instance, at the choice of hand-crafted ear-rings.

Opening hours

Most stores are open from 9 or 10 a.m., markets from 6 a.m. Closing times are mostly at 18 hrs. (20 hrs for food departments); and 20 hrs on Thursdays, 13 hrs on Saturdays. Basic supermarkets are open from 7-20 hrs; Saturday 7-14 hrs.

All are closed on Sundays except for morning markets in some suburban areas.

Department Stores and Shopping Centres

Luxus Department Store, Vörösmarty tér
Aranypók Department Store, Váci Street
Florián Shopping Centre, III Florián tér 6-9
Skála Co-op Department Store, XI Október 23 u. 6-10
Sugar Shopping Centre, XIV Örs vezér tér
Skála-Metro, Nyugati tér – opposite Western Railway Station

You can also purchase a select range of Hungarian goods in International tourist shops. These are mainly located in hotels and accept only hard currency or credit cards.

Folk Art: shops in hotels; or at Folk Art Shop (Népmüvészeti bolt) V, Váci út 14; or XIII Szt István krt 26.

Markets

In search of local colour (and local produce), most people enjoy visiting a bustling market to glimpse everyday life among average Hungarians. Several excellent markets are scattered through Budapest.

Easily the most interesting and accessible is the **Central Marketing Hall** in District IX, at Vámház körút 103. Hundreds of stalls are ranged along six covered avenues, 500 feet long. *See map fig. 12.*

By Western standards, the prices for all the farm and market-garden products seem very low. With flash you can get amusing photos of sausage and salami displays, dairy products, garlic and dangling strings of dazzling-red paprika.

One can reach this central marketing place by taking a No. 2 tram along the river embankment, and get off at Szabadság Bridge. The Central Marketing Hall is then just across the square. Highly recommended!

5.9 Eating out

The Hungarian people enjoy life and this is especially evident when it comes to eating and drinking. Even smaller restaurants offer menus with up to 50 or 60 items every day. All the great specialities of Central Europe and the Balkans are available.

The food is excellent, and served in generous portions at low prices by West European standards. Service is quick and friendly.

Tourist menus

All eating places must offer at least two set menus each day, by law. These inexpensive tourist menus generally include soup, a main course and dessert. However, you will rarely find a translation, and waiters prefer to lure you into the à la carte side of the menu.

Service charge is not usually included in the price unless indicated on the menu and a minimum 15% tip is customary. Many restaurants feature live music during the evening – mainly gipsy violinists who play from table to table, and expect a 500-Forint banknote at each stop.

Here's a rough guide to prices:
Something like 1000 Forints to 2500 for an average set menu. Soups cost from 150 Ft depending on the restaurant, and the ingredients. Fish soup is at the more expensive end.

Starters go from 100 to 800 or 900 Ft. The most expensive starters are goose liver, or Russian caviar. Salads go from 100 Ft. Main courses are especially variations on pork, with a price-range from 800 to 1200 Ft.

Wines: the most expensive is Tokaj, costing 600 to 800 Ft for a half-litre bottle. Other wines in standard size bottles go from 350 to 1000 Ft in a restaurant.

Hungary has more visitors speaking German than any other language, so that's the usual second language. Many menus have only a German translation. But more up-market eating places also have English menus, and waiters who can cope with English.

For a simple lunch, there are hundreds of low-cost fast-food and self-service establishments around town, where you can look and point. Bakeries make up very tempting sandwiches and portions of pizza.

For a more memorable meal, here's a short list of restaurants that serve traditional food. Reservations are recommended at weekends.

District I. – Castle District

Most of the restaurants in this area cater specially for the tourist trade, with plenty of atmosphere, multi-lingual waiters and gipsy musicians.

Fortuna, I., Hess András tér 4   Tel: 1756 857
One of the oldest and most elegant in the castle district,
by the Hilton Hotel. The first book printed in Hungary
was published here in 1473, and the building later housed
the University Press. Open: 12-16 & 19-01 hrs.

Régi Országház, I., Országhaz utca 17   Tel: 1750 650
"The Old Parliament Building", near Hilton Hotel. On
the ground floor it's a regular restaurant serving Hungarian dishes with gipsy music. Downstairs is a wine-cellar
offering extremely simple food.

Alabárdos Restaurant, I., Országház utca 2
In a 16th Century building by the Hilton Hotel, an elegant first-class candle-lit restaurant with medieval furnishings. Open: 19-24 hrs.   Tel: 1560 851

Aranyszarvas, I., Szarvas tér 1   Tel: 1756 451
"The Golden Deer" specialises in venison and other
game, on Buda side near Elizabeth Bridge.

District V. – Inner City
*All the principal hotels have excellent dining rooms,
with first-class service. In the surrounding streets, numerous good restaurants cater for visitors and locals
alike.*

Restaurant Pilvax, V., Pilvax Köz 1-3   Tel: 1176 396
The original restaurant was a coffee house that was a
meeting place for revolutionary groups. The Hungarian
revolution of 1848 started from here. Open: 12-24 hrs;
Sun 12-16 hrs.

Légrádi testvérek, V., Magyar utca 23   Tel: 1186 804
"The Legradi Brothers" is in a small street near the
Astoria Hotel. Very luxurious and expensive, for trendy
diplomats and rich tourists, with golden spoon service.
Open: 17-24 hrs. Closed Sat & Sun.

Százéves, V., Pesti Barnabás utca 2   Tel: 1183 608
"Century" restaurant, claimed as the oldest in Budapest,
operating in a small building that is a listed monument,
near Váci Street and Elizabeth Bridge. Good food, gipsy
music, traditional atmosphere. Open: 12-24 hrs.

Mátyás Pince, V., Március 15 tér 7   Tel: 1181 650
Established 1904, just by Elizabeth Bridge. Among the
traditional specialities are Bridegroom's Soup, and varied
carp dishes. Music is played every evening by gipsies of
the Sándor Latakos clan. Open: 11-01 hrs.

Off-centre restaurants
Etoile, XIII., Pozsonyi út 4   Tel: 1122 242
Near Margit Bridge, French and national cuisine. First

class atmosphere, turn of the century. Open: 12-15 hrs & 18-01 hrs.

New York, VII., Erzsébet körút 9-11   Tel: 1223 849
A restaurant and coffee house, it's a traditional meeting place for poets and writers, and is famous for Hungarian and international cuisine. Open: 9-22 hrs.

Disznófő, XII., Szilassy utca 18   Tel: 1559 765
"Head of a Wild Boar" between the Buda Hills – hunting-lodge atmosphere with traditional meals.

Gundel Restaurant, XIV., Állatkerti körút 2
In the Heroes Square district, one of the most famous in Budapest serving international and Hungarian cuisine. Gundel pancakes were invented here. Expensive. Open: 12-16 & 19-24 hrs.   Tel: 1221 002

Beer-Halls
A number of Gold Fassl, Tuborg, Gösser and other brand-name beer-halls are spread through Budapest. They serve bottled and draught beer and a range of pub snacks. Here are two that are worth sampling:
Kaltenberg Bavarian Royal Beerhall, IX., Kinizsi utca 30.
Emke, VII., Erzsébet körút 2.

Coffee Bars and Pastry Shops
Hungarians have the coffee and cake habit, just as deeply as the Viennese. Cafés and pastry shops flourish in the city centre.
   Among the pastry specialities, try Rétes – thin pastry or Strudel with choice of fillings: almás (apple); meggyes (sour cherry); mákos (poppy seed); túrós (cottage cheese).
   Pancakes (palacsinta) likewise come with a wide range of fillings. The gourmet speciality is Gundel Palacsinta – filled with a nut and raisin paste, drenched in a creamy chocolate rum sauce and then flambéed.
   For the full rich experience of a Hungarian pastry shop, go to **Gerbeaud,** V., Vörösmarty tér 7. Founded in 1858, Gerbeaud is the most famous café and patisserie in Hungary. Very central, it also serves ice-creams and sandwiches. Usually very busy, with fitful service. Open 9-21 hrs.

Hungarian specialities

Hortobágyi húsos palacsinta	Thin pancakes filled with minced pork stew and dressed with sour cream

Libamáj pástétom	Goose liver paté with brandy
Gulyásleves	Chunks of beef, potatoes,
(goulash soup)	onion, tomatoes and peppers with paprika, caraway seeds and garlic (what is called goulash abroad is actually a meat stew called pörkölt).
Köménymag leves nokedlival	Caraway seed soup with dumplings
Hideg almaleves	Cold apple soup

Main course

Balatoni fogas	Pike-perch (considered a prime delicacy)
Paprika szeletek körözöttel töltve	Sliced green peppers, ewe's cheese, spices and a dash of beer
Fatányéros	Mixed grill; several kinds of meat with garnish and salad served on a platter
Szegedi halászlé	Freshwater bouillabaisse with paprika.
Csikós tokány	Strips of beef braised in diced bacon, onions, sliced pepper and tomatoes served with miniature dumplings
Töltött Káposzta	Soured cabbage leaves stuffed with minced meat and rice cooked with sauerkraut and served with sour cream.
Töltött paprika	Stuffed pepper
Paprikás csirke	Paprika chicken
Rablóhús	Served on a brochette; pork, bacon potatoes and onion
Paprikás krumpli	Paprika potatoes often served with sausages or frankfurters.

Guide to menu items

If the menu has a German translation, you'll probably do better with the menu guide in Chapter One, to avoid the confusion of a less familiar language.

Soups & starters:

Bableves	Bean soup
Bakonyi betyárleves	Outlaw soup
Békacomb	Frogs' legs
Erőleves	Consomme
Gyümölcslé	Fruit juice
Leves	Soup
Húsleves	Meat soup
Húsgombóccal	With meat & dumplings

Main courses & snacks:

Bárányhús	Lamb
Borda	Chop
Borjuhús	Veal
Csirke	Chicken
Csuka	Pike
Disznóhús	Pork
Fasirozott	Meatballs
Felfujt	Soufflé
Fogas	Pike-Perch
Galuska	Dumplings
Gulyásleves	Goulash (soup)
Hal	Fish
Halsaláta	Fish salad
Hús	Meat
Kacsa	Duck
Kappan	Capon
Kolbászfélék	Sausages
Liba	Goose
Marhahús	Beef
Metélt	Noodles
Nyúl	Rabbit
Ponty	Carp
Pörkölt	Stew
Pulyka	Turkey
Ráksaláta	Crab salad
Rizs	Rice
Rostélyos	Stewed steak
Sonka	Ham
Szendvics	Sandwich

Vegetables:

Burgonya	Potatoes
Fokhagyma	Garlic
Főzelék	Vegetables
Gomba	Mushrooms
Hagyma	Onions
Káposzta	Cabbage
Paradicsom	Tomatoes
Saláta	Lettuce or salad
Sárgarépa	Carrots
Sültkrumpli	Chips
Uborka	Cucumber
Vegyesfőzelék	Mixed vegetables
Zeller	Celery
Zöldborsó	Peas

Desserts:

Alma	Apple
Aranygaluska	Sweet dumpling
Ananász	Pineapple
Citrom	Lemon
Cseresznye	Cherries

Eper	Strawberries
Fagylalt	Ice-cream
Görögdinnye	Watermelon
Málna	Raspberries
Meggy	Sour cherries
Narancs	Orange
Őszibarack	Peach
Palacsinta	Pancakes
Ribizli	Red currants
Sárgabarack	Apricot
Sajt	Cheese

Miscellaneous:

Cukor	Sugar
Dió	Walnuts
Édeskömény	Caraway seeds
Kenyér	Bread
Mustár	Mustard
Só	Salt
Vaj	Butter

Drinks:

Ásvány-viz	Mineral water
Bor	Wine
Fröccs	Half-wine, half-soda
Gyümölcslé	Fruit juice
Kapuciner	Capuccino
Szóda-viz	Soda water
Sör	Beer
Tea	Tea
Tej	Milk
Viz	Water

Some cooking terms:

Dinsztelve	Braised
Főve	Broiled
Rántva	Breaded
Sülve	Roasted
Sütve	Fried
Töltött	Stuffed

5.10 Nightlife

Budapest offers nightlife to suit all tastes ranging from opera, ballet, symphony concerts and chamber music to rock and jazz, nightclubs, discos and bars. New theatrical productions are premiered every week.

Most nights Hungarian dancers perform in national costume at the MOM Cultural Centre (XII, Csörsz utca 18) or at the Municipal Cultural Centre (XI, Fehérvári út 47). Tickets are available on the spot, or at the Central Booking Office (VI, Andrássy út 18).

Hungary has a rich culture, and national pride ensures that Liszt, Kodály and Bartók get a frequent hearing – especially those works that are based on folk melodies. Many Austrians come regularly to Budapest for musical events, which are so much less expensive than in Vienna.

Standards are high at the two opera houses and three concert halls. There are opera or ballet performances every night during the winter season. Reserved seats can easily be booked from Vienna.

Otherwise get tickets through your hotel or travel-agency rep; or from the Central Booking Office above. Interticket on (36)-1-2667676 will make credit card bookings.

Music festivals

Every year a two-week Spring Festival is scheduled in late March, with about a thousand different events around the city. When opera houses and concert halls close for the summer, the Margaret Island open-air theatre, amongst others, takes over. The season re-opens late September onwards with autumn Music Weeks.

Budapest by night

A popular tourist entertainment is dinner at a traditional restaurant with goulash, strudel, Hungarian wines, folk-lore displays and gipsy music.

The musicians do their soulful best, with languishing gipsy melody, to reduce the entire clientele to wistful melancholia. Then, when the tears are almost ready to flow, they set you afire with a whirling, exciting folk-dance. Not to be missed!

River cruises

Another variation on the goulash party theme is to take an evening Danube Cruise with dinner, wine, music and folklore show. At first the cost may seem rather high. But you travel on a very comfortable boat and the gipsy band is first-class – normally a lead violin, a cello, a cymbalom, a clarinet and a base.

As Budapest lights up, you get fine views of a capital that sparkles. Other evening cruises are available, with or without music or food.

Nightclubs, cabarets and discos

Most of the leading hotels feature a choice of night enter-tainment. Check what's currently on offer at the Atrium Hyatt, the Marriott, Hotel Emke, Astoria Hotel, Kempin-ski Hotel Corvinus, Mercure Buda, Hotel Aquincum, or the Hotel Flamenco.

There is also wide choice of smaller establishment which wax or wane in popularity. Some are extremely sleazy, and are best avoided. Again, check locally on the current scene.

5.11 At your service

Money & Banking
The Hungarian currency is the forint (Ft). Coins are 10, 20, 50 and 100 Ft. Notes are 500, 1,000 and 5,000 Ft.

Changing money
The exchange rate is not the same everywhere. Check at the Hungarian National Bank, National Savings Bank (OTP) branches, exchange desks at travel and tourist offices and at hotels. Banking hours are normally Monday to Friday 9-17 hrs; Saturdays 9-14 hrs. In high season, you can also change money at the Posta Bank on Saturdays and Sundays, from 9-13 hrs.

Black market con-men
Produce your passport when changing money. Street deals with private citizens are not legal, and light-fingered black marketeers could easily leave you holding a bundle of toilet paper.

Keep your exchange dockets. On leaving Hungary you may re-exchange only a maximum of half the amount indicated on receipts.

Post Office and Telephone
Opening hours – generally from 8-18 hours Monday to Friday and 8-12 hrs on Saturdays. Main offices operate from 7-20 hrs.

Stamps can be bought quicker from tobacconists, Monday to Friday. Post boxes are painted red and mail is collected every few hours.

Other services offered by the post office are telephone, telegraph and telex services. Phone cards are available at post offices and tobacconists.

International phone calls: insert at least 100 Ft coin in the slot. For dialling codes, see section 1.3 of this book. An international telecommunications centre operates from 7-20 hrs Monday to Friday and until 19 hrs on Saturdays at the corner of Petőfi Sándor utca and Martinelli tér (Budapest V). Linguists are also on duty here.

For directory enquiries in English, phone 1172-200.

Calls within Budapest: insert a 20 Ft coin in the slot and dial the number. Daytime city phones give you three minutes for 20 Forints. From 18 hrs till 7 a.m. you get six minutes for 20 Ft.

Other phone numbers, and addresses
Police Headquarters, also dealing with passports
1061 Budapest VI, Andrássy út 12
Emergency Police phone 107; Fire 105; Ambulance 104

Lost Property
Central lost property office
Bp. V Erzsébet tér 5. Tel: 1174-961   Open: Mon 8-18 hrs; Tues to Thurs 8-17; Fri 8-15; Sat closed.

Losses on Public Transport:
BKV office, Bp. VII Akácfa u 18   Tel: 1226-613
Open: Mon, Tue & Thu 7-16 hrs; Wed & Fri 7-18.30. Passports and other personal documents handed into the Lost Property Office are transferred to KEOKH (Aliens Registration Office) at Police HQ – address above.

Medical
Budapest is one of Europe's leading spa cities. Many people come to regain their health at one of the therapeutic baths. However, in case of an accident or sudden illness the Hungarian National Health Service (S.Z.T.K.) and the emergency squad (Mentők) are very capable of handling any unexpected problems.

Most Hungarian doctors and dentists also have private practices, at which payment is required for consultations. Keep receipts for any travel insurance claim. To find an English-speaking doctor or dentist, ask at hotel reception. Your consulate can also name suitable local doctors.

Pharmaceutical chemists
Look for the sign *gyógyszertár* or *patika*. These shops only sell pharmaceutical and related products. For toiletries go to an *illatszerbolt* and for films to a *fotószaküzlet*. Some chemists remain open all night. Their addresses can be found on a sign displayed in other chemists' windows.
24-hour service:
91 Teréz Körút 1067   22 Frankel Leo út 1027
86 Rákóczi út 1074   3 Boráros tér 1093

Embassies
Great Britain, V Harmincad u 6   Tel: 1182-888
USA, Szabadság tér 12   Tel: 1124-224
Canada, II Budakeszi út 53/d   Tel: 1165-858

Tourist Information
For information in English call TOURINFORM on 1179-800. The service operates from 7-21 hrs Monday to Friday; to 20 hrs on Saturdays and 8-13 hrs on Sundays. The office is located at Sütő u. 2, next to Deák Square.

News
The Hungarians broadcast an English language service called Radio Bridge on FM 102.1. It's a round-the-clock programme which carries the Voice of America news reports and features. Buy the *Budapest Sun* and *Budapest Week* for news and listings.

Chapter Six

Poland

6.1 Rebirth of a nation

A visitor to Poland cannot escape from the drama of Polish history, filled with wars and invasions. For centuries Poland was a major player in Eastern Europe, with boundaries that once reached from the Baltic to the Black Sea. There have been constant problems from the big neighbours, Russia and Germany. But even the Swedes figure among invaders from the past, along with the Teutonic Knights, Tartars and Turks.

The last king of independant Poland was Stanislaw Augustus Poniatowski. In his time, Poland lost its independence in the 1790s, being finally split three ways. Russia took Warsaw and the eastern provinces, Austria had Kraków and the south, while Prussia took the west.

A rebellion against Russian rule in 1830 was rigorously suppressed, with mass deportations to Siberia. Many patriots, including Chopin, migrated especially to France. Subsequent uprisings likewise collapsed.

During the 19th century, education in the eastern provinces was Russified, while a parallel policy was followed when Prussia joined the German Reich and schools were Germanized in 1872. In the Austrian third of the country, the rule was relatively liberal, and many intellectuals migrated to Kraków.

Meanwhile the rural population was poverty stricken and illiterate. Millions emigrated mainly to USA between 1890 and 1914. The 'Polish Question' was a recurrent subject of international debate.

During World War I, the political and military manoeuvres became ever more complicated as the battles swung back and forth across Polish territory. Finally, in 1918, the three former rulers of divided Poland – Austria, Prussia and Russia – had all lost the war. November 11 was the day of Poland's resurrection and return to independence, back on the European map roughly to the borders of 1772.

That independence continued until the infamous agreement between Hitler and Stalin, leading to invasion in September 1939 by Germany and the Soviet Union. The

112

sad fate of Poland and its people is among the blackest chapters of the 20th century.

But the Poles are resilient. In the latest pendulum swing to their history, July 1997 saw President Clinton making a speech in Warsaw's historic centre, welcoming the prospect of Poland joining NATO. And Poland is currently on the short list for joining the European Union, with the government pushing hard to gain entry.

Poland today is a cheerful country. Warsaw has been resurrected, and the city is lively with an expanding economy that is shaking off the torpor of the past. The finest buildings of old-time Warsaw have long since been totally rebuilt in their original style. In fact, the restoration of the Old Town was the priority of the immediate postwar period. Apart from much of the Soviet-style architecture, historic Warsaw can rank among the most beautiful capitals of Europe.

The River Vistula – flowing from southern Poland through Kraków to Warsaw and thence to the Baltic port of Gdansk (formerly Danzig) – is the historic trading route which links by canal to the waterway systems of Belarus, Ukraine and Russia.

It was Kraków's initial prosperity as a trading centre that first gave the city a leading position among Polish towns, and thence to becoming the Polish capital in mid-11th century. That function continued until the capital was transferred in 1596 to the more central city of Warsaw.

In the 20th century Kraków had the unbelievable good fortune of totally escaping war damage, leaving an untouched historic centre which is listed as a World Heritage Site.

Kraków is an old town, but young in spirit thanks to a ten percent population of University students. In May, students hold a youth pageant called Juvenalia, with singing, dancing, drama and the election of a Student Beauty Queen. The most famous former student of the University is Pope John Paul II.

Everyone loves Kraków and its spacious Market Square which is the focal point of medieval streets that haven't changed over the centuries. It is Poland's most popular tourist destination.

6.2 Planning the trip

Entry formalities are minimal. No visa is required by British, West European or US citizens.

When to go? Winter is extremely chilly, and even April and October are cool enough for heavy clothing. May to September are the most pleasant months, but rainwear is still needed.

In recent years LOT Polish Airlines has spent $800 million on new Boeing 737s and 767s, and claims to operate Europe's most modern fleet. Numerous direct flights serve Warsaw from Heathrow and Manchester; and several flights weekly from Gatwick to Kraków.

British Airways likewise operates from Heathrow and Manchester to Warsaw, and Gatwick to Kraków.

6.3 Internal transport

Warsaw and Kraków can easily be linked in a two-centre package, with a 2½-hour express train service through typical Polish farming countryside.

Both cities are well served by frequent low-cost buses and trams. As in other Central European countries, you buy tickets in advance from kiosks and at hotel newspaper counters. For the equivalent of about 20p (one Zloty) you can ride any distance – even to the airport. Just cancel a ticket in the validating machine inside your tram or bus. It's worth noting the numbers of trams and buses that pass near your hotel, so that you can hop on even for relatively short distances.

Taxis are metered, and rates are modest. A short journey will cost only about £1. However, beware of the taxi Mafia who lurk at airports and around the principal hotels. The most honest taxis are those with a well-displayed phone number, and the price per kilometre painted on the vehicle.

6.4 Learn a little Polish?

Similar to Czech and Russian, Polish is a Slav language which look like a tongue-twister's nightmare. If you haven't previously tangled with a Slav language, best advice for a few days in Poland is to rely on the universal spread of English or German among everyone in contact with tourism.

However, here are some hints on pronouncing some of those place-names with peculiar accents.

The letter 'ł' or 'Ł' is pronounced 'w' as in 'wind'. So Warsaw's Łazienki Park is pronounced Wazienki.

The letter 'w' is pronounced 'v'. So Kraków comes out as Krak-of.

cz is the Polish way of spelling the 'ch' sound, as in children. And sz becomes 'sh' as in ship.

dżem is pronounced as gem. c is pronounced as 'ts'. So Plac is like Platz in German.

If you're reading a street map, ul. stands for ulica, meaning Street; Al. for Aleja – Avenue; Plac for Square; Rynek for Market Square.

Yes is tak; no is nie. Good morning or afternoon is dzień dobry. Good night is dobranoc. Please is Proszę. Thank you is Dziękuję.

6.5 Polish cuisine

Traditional cuisine is based on old-time peasant food, with wide choice of soups and stews. An average restaurant can list ten different soups on the menu. Bigos is in top rank: a hunter's stew of sauerkraut, dried mushrooms, sausages, bacon and other meats such as venison.

There are numerous variations on pork or poultry, including goose, duck and turkey. Polish ham is excellent. A favourite fish is carp. Mushrooms, beetroot, cabbage and cauliflower are among the usual choice of vegetables, possibly with stuffed dumplings. The former widespread Jewish cuisine still survives, with chicken cutlet, chicken livers or carp cooked in Jewish style.

Desserts run the gamut from cakes to ice cream. Cheese is not normally served after a main course.

Tea and coffee usually appear without milk.

In the hard drinks department, Polish vodka is excellent. Beer is the most popular refreshment, and is very low-cost compared with UK prices. Hungarian and Bulgarian wines are readily available, but French imports are much higher priced.

6.6 Sunday in Poland

Shops are closed, but museums are all open (mostly closed Monday) and sightseeing tours and excursions are fully operative. Most interesting is to attend a service in one of the principal churches, which will almost certainly be totally packed with standing room only for late-comers. Poland is now 97% Roman Catholic. (Prewar, before the Holocaust, 28% of the populations of Warsaw and Kraków were Jewish). Even during the Communist era, churches were always full.

From Warsaw, Sunday is the best day for visiting the birthplace of Chopin at Żelazowa Wola, with the chance of hearing an on-the-spot piano recital.

6.7 Shopping

Shop hours are mostly 11-19 hrs Mon-Fri; 9-13 hrs Sat. But tourist shops and kiosks often keep more variable hours. Most stores are happy to accept major credit cards. Around the obvious tourist focal points there are plentiful shops that sell maps, illustrated guide books, antiques, costume dolls, folk-art, paintings, glass, silver and amber jewellery. CDs are cheap, and are often pirated copies from Bulgaria.

No works of art produced before 1945 may be exported without prior permission.

POLAND

Poland's Baltic shores are the world's richest source of amber, found in sands that are 40 to 60 million years old. Amber prices compare very favourably with the product in the West. Don't buy from street vendors who may offer plastic imitations.

6.8 At your service

Money & Banking

Don't buy zloties in Britain, as you'll get a better rate on arrival in Poland. The exchange rate is freely floating. Because of inflation, the revalued zloty at 4 to the pound sterling in 1995 had reached 6 zloty to the pound by late 1997 when this book was printed. For the visitor, this means that Polish prices for meals, drinks, local transport and entertainment seem very cheap.

You can change at the arrival airport, banks (open 8-18 hrs Mon-Fri), your hotel or at street kiosks and currency exchange bureaux labelled Kantor. They all deduct minimal commission. In fact the Kantor offer some of the best deals, as many charge no commission. They just live off the modest spread between buying and selling rates.

At the departure airport, you can re-exchange your surplus Polish money. Don't take zloties back home, where you'll lose badly on exchange.

Incidentally, some 'old' zloty banknotes are still circulating. Ten thousand old zloty equal one new zloty. They are easily recognised by having at least four zeroes. Refuse to accept them, if they are given in your change.

One new zloty splits into 100 groszy.

Telephone

If you don't want to use the hotel for international calls, buy a telephone card for minimum charge of under £1 for 25 local calls. To use a phone card, first tear off the top left corner where it is already perforated. Otherwise it cannot be accepted by the phone machine.

Public Holidays

Jan 1; Easter Monday; May 1 & 3; Corpus Christi (Thursday June 11 in 1998); Aug 15; Nov 1 & 11; Dec 24 & 25. Some museums are open on public holidays, but close the day after. Check locally!

Polish National Tourist Offices

Remo House, 310-312 Regent St., London W1R 5AJ. Open Mon-Fri 10-17 hrs.
Tel: 0171-580 5037. Fax: 0171-323 0774.

500 Fifth Avenue, Suite 408, New York 10017.
Tel: 212-869 1074.

The Mutual Group Center, 3300 Bloor St. W., Suite 3080, Toronto, Canada. Tel: 416-236 4242.

Chapter Seven

Warsaw

7.1 A capital rebuilt

The recorded history of Warsaw started 700 years ago, when the first buildings were erected on a hill overlooking the river. The area was then surrounded by medieval fortifications like the red-brick walls seen today, with a moat, towers, drawbridges to the gates, and a barbican which guarded the northern gate.

By the year 1596, Warsaw was still just a small provincial town covered by the present-day Old Town enclosed by the city walls, together with a settlement called New Town just outside the walls.

However, Warsaw had the advantage of a more central and convenient location in this huge country, which was then three times bigger than contemporary Poland. Thanks to a union between Lithuania, Poland and Ukraine, the country stretched from the Black Sea to the Baltic. Warsaw was just halfway.

So, 400 years ago, King Zygmunt III Waza relocated the capital from Kraków to Warsaw. Despite all the subsequent ups and downs of history, Warsaw continued to grow with new streets, parks and gardens, the palaces of the aristocracy and the substantial houses of the wealthy middle class.

During the 19th century, while under Russian rule, a railway linked Warsaw with Vienna and St Petersburg. Industry expanded, serving markets throughout Russia.

Today, after 50 years of rebuilding the city from the ruins of 1944, Warsaw flourishes as a vibrant business centre – a launch-pad for trade with the countries of the former Soviet Union. All the big multinational companies are well established here, and the former headquarters of the Communist Party are used as a Stock Exchange. There is feverish construction of more and more high-rise hotels, offices and banks. Effectively Warsaw has become the trading hub of Eastern Europe.

For the City Break visitor, the attraction of Warsaw lies in the beautiful Old Town, the splendid palaces, mansions and parks, and in the links with Chopin. The year is filled with music, from classical to jazz.

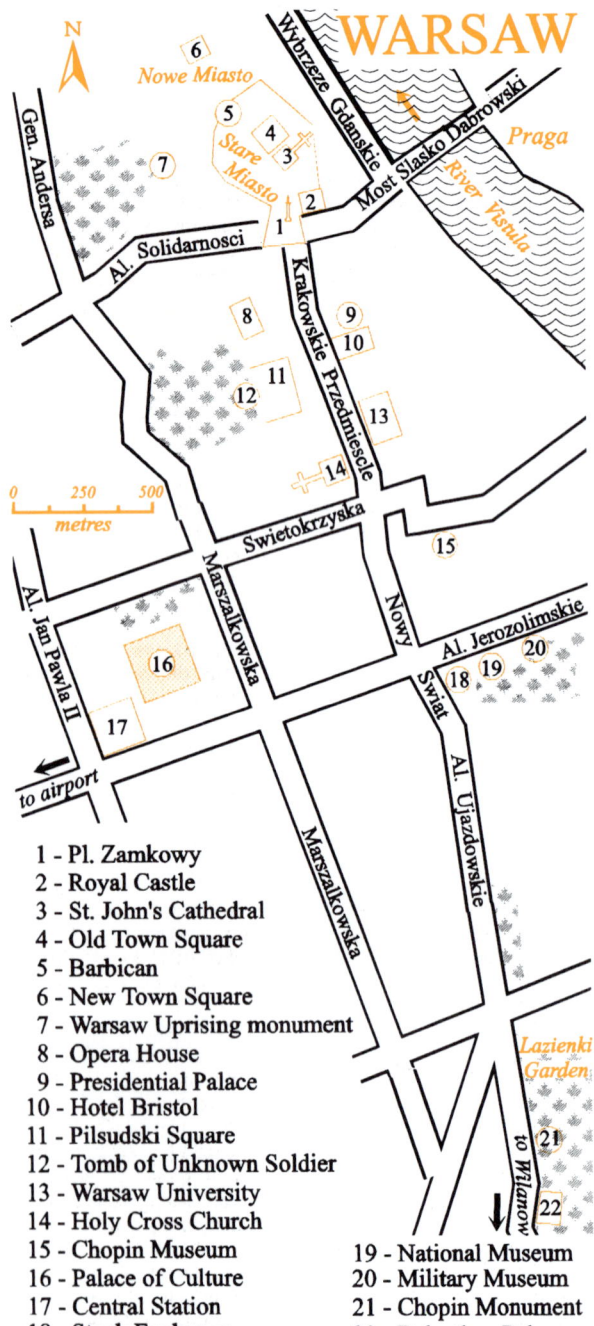

1 - Pl. Zamkowy
2 - Royal Castle
3 - St. John's Cathedral
4 - Old Town Square
5 - Barbican
6 - New Town Square
7 - Warsaw Uprising monument
8 - Opera House
9 - Presidential Palace
10 - Hotel Bristol
11 - Pilsudski Square
12 - Tomb of Unknown Soldier
13 - Warsaw University
14 - Holy Cross Church
15 - Chopin Museum
16 - Palace of Culture
17 - Central Station
18 - Stock Exchange
19 - National Museum
20 - Military Museum
21 - Chopin Monument
22 - Belvedere Palace

7.2 Arrival and hotel

Most hotels are located in the Central area, six miles from the airport. An honest metered taxi charges about £4, but the taxi Mafia can demand three or four times that figure. Budget watchers could choose the airport bus costing £1 with stops at a number of leading hotels, including Novotel, Marriott and Bristol.

7.3 Orientation

Warsaw is spread across both sides of the Vistula River. The essential Warsaw is on the west bank. Across the bridges is Praga, a residential and industrial area with very little of tourist interest.

The dominating landmark of the Central district, the commercial area around Central Railway Station, is the 758-ft skyscraper Palace of Culture and Science, a 1950s gift from Stalin, built in his favourite Moscow wedding-cake style. It's a useful point of orientation, but is an otherwise unloved memento of the Communist past. *See map on previous page, fig. 16.*

Jerusalem Avenue – Aleja Jerozolimskie – is a broad artery that is joined by traffic from the airport, past Central Station and the Marriott Hotel, and thence east-wards to a major bridge over the Vistula.

Another major avenue called Marszałkowska carves the Central district from south to north, where it meets Solidarity Avenue – Al. Solidarności. The great tourist highlights are concentrated close by, in the walled Old Town, called Stare Miasto. Entry into the pedestrianized Old Town is mainly across Plac Zamkowy (*see map fig. 1*), the Castle Square distinguished by a tall column topped by King Zygmunt, who made Warsaw the capital.

Due south from Castle Square runs the Royal Way, past the Bristol Hotel and the splendid aristocratic palaces and mansions built during Poland's Golden Age. This highway links the former official royal residence in the Castle to the private Wilanów Palace 8 miles away.

Using public transport, it's easy to reach the Old Town, and then spend hours wandering around. The Royal Way is best seen first on a sightseeing tour that includes Wilanów Palace. You can then use public transport to explore some areas in more detail – such as the shopping street called Nowy Świat, or Łazienki Park.

For a trip out of town, the most rewarding choice is a coach tour during summer to Chopin's birthplace at Żela-zowa Wola, with a Sunday recital in the family garden.

The itinerary includes Brochów, the typical Polish village where Chopin's parents were married and Chopin was baptized; and Niepokalanów, where a Franciscan monastery has become a major centre of pilgrimage.

7.4 Basic Warsaw – the Old Town

Castle Square (Plac Zamkowy) centres on the column of King Zygmunt III Waza, who enlarged the adjoining Castle and converted it into the official royal residence. Over the centuries, the building has been pillaged, burnt and destroyed several times. But it's now fully restored, with interiors reconstructed and valuable art-works back in place. Well worth visiting! *See map figs. 1 & 2.*

Peek over the city walls, down into the former moat, and you can picture the original strength of these medieval fortifications. Only the darker bricks are original.

From Castle Square, Świętojańska Street leads past **St John's Cathedral** (*map fig. 3),* founded in 1370 and rebuilt in 1956. Whenever Pope John Paul II came to Warsaw, he attended this church. Here is buried Cardinal Wyszyński, who played a major role during the postwar years in relations between Church and State.

Only a few steps further along is the **Old Town Market Square** (*fig. 4),* a triumph of reconstruction in the early postwar period. Every detail was copied from old photos and paintings into a reproduction of the original 17th and 18th century structure. Each building has its interest, with frescoes inspired by history or legend.

Year-round, this lively centre is thronged with visitors, with entertainment provided by street musicians and fast-portrait artists. During summer, restaurants and cafés function outdoors beneath coloured umbrellas. Painters cluster with their works on one side of the square, while almost every building features a basement tavern, a shop, restaurant or mini museum.

Each street that radiates from the square is likewise packed with photogenic architecture, charming eating places, antique stores and jewellers.

Past the north side of the market square leads out to the 16th-century **Barbican Tower** (*fig. 5),* now occupied by craft workshops and art galleries. Here is a popular statue of Warsaw's legendary mermaid, in fighting mood.

Old Warsaw was very small. People began to build new houses outside the walls, calling their satellite settlement the **New Town** (*fig. 6)* – now 600 years old.

The most famous former resident of New Town was the Nobel Prize-winner, Madame Curie, born as Maria Skłodowska in 1867 at 16 Freta Street. The house is now a biographical **Madame Curie Museum**. She is the first woman to be buried in the Pantheon in Paris, as of 1994.

Memorials

In this part of Warsaw are two monuments that testify to the tragic years of Nazi occupation. The dramatic **Monument of the Warsaw Uprising** (*fig. 7)* commemorates the bitter fighting in August and September 1944, when the Polish resistance rose against the Germans. About

200,000 people were killed. The Russian army had reached Praga across the river, but – for whatever political or military reasons – they did not make the crossing until January 1945, when only ruins were left to liberate.

There had been an earlier insurrection, in April 1943. Prewar, Warsaw had 380,000 Jews, comprising 28% of the city's inhabitants – the world's second largest Jewish community after New York. In 1940 the Nazis established a gigantic ghetto, where 450,000 Jews from Warsaw and other towns and villages were concentrated, and surrounded by eleven miles of walls, ten feet high.

Removal to the Treblinka death camp began in 1942. In the following April the Nazis moved in to liquidate the Jews who still remained. They fought back for several weeks. On the 8th of May the uprising ended, when the last remaining leaders committed suicide in their bunker.

Nothing remains of the ghetto walls. But the **Monument to the Heroes of the Ghetto Uprising** at Ludwik Zamenhofa Street (west of General Anders Street) has become a pilgrimage site in memory of those who died.

7.5 The Royal Way

South from Castle Square is the superb highway lined with historic buildings. It doubles as a Chopin trail, with numerous reminders of Poland's most famous composer.

Past the statue of Adam Mickiewicz – Poland's national poet and close friend of Chopin – is the **Presidential Palace** (see map fig. 9), which originally was the 17th-century Radziwiłł Palace where Chopin frequently gave recitals as a boy. The Radziwiłłs were a very rich family who owned half of Lithuania. Postwar the palace was nationalized and used for diplomatic meetings. In 1955, the Warsaw Pact was signed here. In 1989, talks were held with Lech Walensa, leading to free elections.

Next door is the famous **Bristol Hotel** (fig. 10), built 100 years ago and mainly funded by the wealthy pianist Paderewski, who became Premier of Poland in 1919.

Behind the more elderly Europejski Hotel opposite is **Piłsudski Square** (fig. 11) named after the nationalist statesman who dominated inter-war Poland. During German occupation, the square was renamed as Adolf Hitler Platz. The square opens towards the Saski Gardens, where a palace once stood. **The Tomb of the Unknown Soldier** (fig. 12) is backed by columns that remain from the destroyed palace.

The north end of the square is occupied by the **Opera House** (fig. 8), one of the largest in Europe, seating 1,900 people. Best tickets cost £6.

Back on the Royal Way, the baroque **Church and Cloister of the Nuns of the Visitation** was one of the few buildings which survived the war intact. At age 14, Chopin was appointed as the church organist. Chopin's

French father taught French literature at a neighbouring school for aristocrats. He lived just down the road in the first floor of an annex to the late-baroque **Czapski Palace**, where a drawing-room museum can be visited. The Palace now houses the **Academy of Fine Arts**. The buildings opposite form part of **Warsaw University** *(fig. 13)*.

Chopin left Warsaw in 1830, shortly before a revolt against Russian rule. He never returned, but formed part of the nationalist emigré group in Paris. His music reflected the music of the countryside where he was born, at Żelazowa Wola, 32 miles from Warsaw. After Chopin's death, only his heart came back to Poland, to the **Holy Cross Church** *(fig. 14)* close to his former home.

In the road close by stands a statue of the astronomer, **Copernicus**. The highway changes name to Nowy Świat (New World), and is lined with up-market shops. On summer weekends, the street is often closed off and pedestrianised, and outdoor cafés occupy the roadway. The pastry shop called A. Blikle is famed for doughnuts.

Closer to the Vistula is **Ostrogski Palace** *(fig. 15)*, housing the museum and concert hall of the Chopin Society. Behind the Palace is the **Chopin Music Academy**.

Back on the Royal Way, the road crosses Aleja Jerozolimskie, where the former Communist Party HQ is now a temple of capitalism, with banks and a Stock Exchange *(fig. 18)*. Along the Avenue is the **National Museum** with fine collections of ancient, medieval and modern art. The adjacent **Army Museum** shows weapons from 10th century to World War II. *See figs. 19 & 20.*

Meanwhile, the Royal Way continues south through an elegant neighbourhood of embassies, villas, the **Botanical Gardens** and **Łazienki Park**. The best time for visiting the Park is Sunday afternoon, when summertime Chopin concerts are held in front of a remarkable monument *(fig. 21)* of the composer beneath a symbolic weeping willow tree. Evening Chopin recitals are often given in the **Orangerie court theatre** of the **Royal Palace on Water**.

Next along the Royal Way is **Belvedere Palace**, the former official Presidential residence last used by Lech Walensa. It's now a VIP guest-house. *See map fig. 22.*

Finally, past dormitory suburbs of postwar gruesome style, the highway reaches **Wilanów Palace** where King Jan III Sobieski built his private residence 300 years ago. A complete tour – entrance £2 but closed Tuesday – is one of Warsaw's great highlights, showing the aristocratic lifestyle of three centuries ago. Don't miss it!

A final viewpoint

For an overall view of Warsaw, ride to the 30th floor of the 37-storey Palace of Culture and Science *(fig. 16)*. Various learned institutions are still based here. But a 3,000-seat hall built for Communist Party congresses is now used for concerts and jazz festivals; and there's a casino. It's doubtful whether Stalin would have approved.

Chapter Eight

Krakow

8.1 Introduction to Kraków

In contrast to Warsaw, Kraków suffered no destruction during the war. Today it's a city of 750,000 inhabitants, of whom 64,000 are students at Europe's third oldest university. In 1978 the beautiful city centre went on UNESCO's list of World Heritage Sites.

The Polish joke is that Warsaw is the political capital of Poland, but Kraków is the tourist and pub capital. There are 70-odd pubs in the centre of the Old Town, many in medieval cellars which stay open till the last customer goes home. With so many visitors and students, there is lively nightlife where costs are low.

Everything focusses on the Market Square, among the biggest in Europe, 200 metres by 200 metres. The layout dates from 1257. Here you can enjoy your sightseeing sitting down in an outdoor café, letting the atmosphere wash over you, and enjoying the pleasure of people watching. In this prime tourist spot, a beer costs half what you'd pay in an average English pub.

You can even do some photography sitting down, taking pictures of the Town Hall tower, of the medieval Cloth Hall rebuilt in 16th century, and of rival outdoor cafés and their coloured umbrellas and fences of flowers. There are no traffic fumes, as only a few service vehicles like taxis are permitted inside the Old Town.

Every hour from the watchtower of the Church of Our Lady, a bugle sounds forth, to end strangled in mid-note. It's all in support of the 14th-century legend of a sentry who sounded the alarm of a Tartar attack, only to be slain by an enemy arrow in the throat.

Capital of Poland from 1040 until 1596, central Kraków is packed with solid buildings that date from the city's Golden Age of the 15th and 16th centuries. It's all concentrated within a few hundred yards of the Market Square. There are eating places galore, ranging from Poland's oldest restaurant Wierzynek, established 1364 at Rynek Główny 16 on a corner of the Square, to simple cafeterias that can give a hearty lunch inside £2.

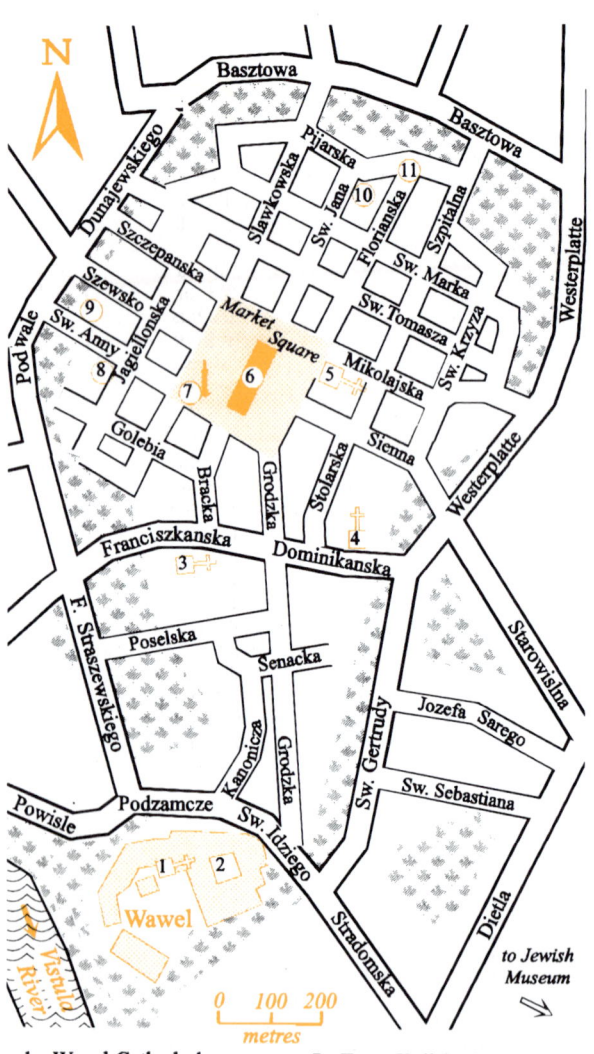

1 - Wavel Cathedral
2 - Wavel Castle
3 - Franciscan Church
4 - Dominican Church
5 - Church of Our Lady
6 - Cloth Hall

7 - Town Hall Tower
8 - Collegium Mauis
9 - St Anne's Church
10 - Czartoryski Art Museum
11 - Barbican
11 - St Florian's Gate

KRAKOW - Old Town

8.2 Arrival, orientation & transport

In the airport baggage hall you need a German, Austrian or Polish coin to unleash a trolley. From Kraków airport, the 9-mile journey to the centre follows a country-lane route through scenes of strip farming, with each tiny plot carrying a different crop.

Transport cost is about £6 or £7 by taxi, or less than 25p by frequent public bus 152, 208 or D. LOT publishes a local timetable with the exact bus timings.

The historic heart of medieval Kraków was ringed by double defensive walls, 47 towers, seven entrance gates and a moat. The walls were replaced last century by a broad green belt of parks and gardens called the **Planty**, which now serves as the limit of the traffic-free zone.

The Market Square called Rynek Główny is reached by a grid pattern of magnificent cobbled streets that are unchanged from centuries past. Each corner of the square led to a gate with a tower. The main artery – Floriańska Street to Rynek Główny and then along Grodzka – was the Royal Way. The medieval kings entered the city at the Barbican en route to their fortified palace, the Wawel, which overlooks a curve of the Vistula River.

Owing to very strict planning laws, post-war hotels have been built just outside the Old Town centre, along the avenues that radiate like wheel spokes from the hub.

Trams and buses ply along these traffic arteries and follow the ring road around the Planty. Buy some tickets, less than 20p each, and it's worth taking even short rides to and around the Old Town.

8.3 Basic Krakow - the Old Town

Let's start with the former power centre of Kraków - Wawel Hill. During the Neolithic and Bronze Ages, 4,500-750 BC, the limestone rock was a craft and trading centre. By the 11th century AD, Wawel was the fortified base of the princes who became rulers of all Poland.

From the Market Square, Wawel is reached along Grodzka Street, and then up a steep cobbled hill which echoed in the past to the carriage horses of the Polish kings and their followers. A baroque entrance gate leads to the **Cathedral**, the Polish Westminster Abbey, where kings were crowned, and later buried. From the 19th century, the Cathedral also became the burial place for national heroes and poets. *See Kraków map fig. 1.*

Kraków became a centre of Christianity around 1000 AD, when the cathedral was founded. A fire in 1305 led to the present-day replacement completed in 1364. The Sigismund Chapel is regarded as the most beautiful Renaissance chapel in Europe. In the Sigismund Tower, a massive bell cast in 1520 is rung on national occasions.

Wavel Castle

The official residence of the Polish kings until they moved the capital to Warsaw, today's Royal Palace was built after the original burnt down in the 15th century. In the 16th century, Wawel was Europe's biggest castle built in Renaissance style. *See map fig. 2.*

Because of the difference in climate, there is much difference between Polish and Italian Renaissance. For instance, the days are very short in Poland from November to February. Hence, architects built larger windows to prolong the working day. In Italy the main working floor is usually the ground floor which would have more shade and be cooler. In Poland, the working floor is upstairs, to capture more sunlight. Buildings have steeper rooves because of the snow and rain; and very thick walls, to keep warm during winter.

Visitors wear plastic slippers to protect the polished floors on a guided tour through the apartments. Everything is in authentic period. Art works and 16th-century Flemish tapestries had been evacuated for safety to Canada, so most of the furnishings and decorations survived the years of German occupation. Frescoes below the ceiling and the painted and gilded columns and beams have been restored to their original glowing colours.

Back towards Market Square, **Ulitsa Kanonitza** runs roughly parallel with Grodzka, and is the most beautiful Renaissance street of Kraków.

The only tramlines in the Old Town cross Franciszkańska and Dominikańska Streets, each with its church and monastery founded in the 13th century. Pope John Paul II lived from 1964 to 1978 in the Bishop's Palace opposite the Franciscan Church. *See map fig. 3.*

Market Square

In the square, virtually every building offers decorative or historic interest. Overlooking the square is the **Church of Our Lady** *(fig. 5)* in the north-east corner, rebuilt in 14th century Gothic style with many Baroque additions. The interior decorations and furnishings are superb, with beautiful wall paintings and masterly carvings of the main altar and pews. Services are always extremely crowded.

On the square outside are delightful flower stalls and a statue of Adam Mickiewicz, Poland's favourite poet, who is buried in the Cathedral. Postage stamps are sold from an old Post Office mail-coach. Cards and letters posted in the coach will be stamped with decorative data. Office hours are 9-16 hrs.

The **Cloth Hall** *(fig. 6)* occupying the centre of the square was redesigned in the 16th century, with arcades added last century. Inside are stalls that sell folk handicrafts and souvenirs. Upstairs, the gallery of 19th-century Polish painting forms part of the National Museum.

In the 19th century, Kraków's population was greatly reduced when the city under Austrian rule lost its former importance. The 14th-century **Town Hall** was demolished, but the **Tower** (*fig. 7*) was left standing. The cellar is now a café and restaurant, full of atmosphere.

Walk up Sw. Anny street and you come to the **Collegium Maius**, with the entrance on Jagiellońska Street. Dating from early 15th century, this is the oldest building of Kraków University. The inner courtyard is charming, with steps leading up to a first-floor balcony. A museum includes the Jagiellonian globe of 1510 which features a first-time showing of America. The university's most famous graduate was Copernicus, whose astronomical instruments are displayed. *See map fig. 8.*

In November 1939, the Nazis arrested 183 professors and sent them to concentration camps. Only 53 returned.

Around the corner is the collegiate **Church of St Anne**, built late 17th century in Baroque style. *See map fig. 9.* There's a monument to Copernicus in the transept, and his statue is close by in the Planty.

On the north side of the Old Town is the **Czartoryski Art Museum** (*fig. 10*) at 19 St. John's Street (Sw. Jana). Its two great treasures are Leonardo's *Lady with Ermine* and Rembrandt's *Landscape with the Good Samaritan.*

Further around the Planty is the **Barbican**, a superb circular fortress built in 1499. Close by is **St Florian's Gate** (*see map fig. 11*) which was the ceremonial royal entrance gate to the city. That remaining part of the city wall is used as a gallery, propping up paintings by young artists. Through the Gate and along Florianska Street leads back to the Market Square.

8.4 Jewish Kazimierz

During medieval times, following numerous persecutions in Western Europe, increasing numbers of Jews resettled in Poland where there were no barriers. In 1335 King Casimir the Great inaugurated a new Jewish town just outside the walls of Kraków. Named Kazimierz after the king, the settlement flourished. During Casimir's reign, the Jews rose to great influence, and grew wealthy in trade and finance. In Kraków itself, another Jewish quarter flourished around the present-day St Anna street.

Neither of these areas was a traditional ghetto, but an area in which the Jewish community chose to live and where several synagogues were clustered. Kazimierz became the largest and most active Jewish centre in Europe, with a distinguished intellectual life.

Another major influx came from Jews expelled from Spain. The Sephardic culture cross-fertilised with the East-European Ashkenazi. Later, Kazimierz was merged into Kraków. Wealthier members of the community lived in the Old Town, while the poor and the Orthodox stayed in Kazimierz. Until the Nazi occupation, Jews comprised over a quarter of Kraków's population.

KRAKOW

During the war, the community was devastated, with mass removal to the Auschwitz-Birkenau death camps. Some escaped thanks to Oskar Schindler's now-famous List of 1200 names. The Steven Spielberg movie was made in the area where the events happened, and Szeroka Street was the setting for some of the film scenes.

Today, the Old Synagogue (the oldest in Poland, built mid-15th century) in Szeroka Street functions as a historical museum dedicated to the Jews who lived in this area till 1941. Otherwise, little remains except for the restored 16th-century Remu'h Synagogue and its graveyard.

Two neighbouring restaurants called Ariel feature Polish-Jewish cuisine. Several times weekly, a Jewish dinner with traditional Yiddish music and folk songs make a memorable and enjoyable evening.

Auschwitz-Birkenau

For a ghastly reminder of past horrors, regular tours visit the State Museum outside the small industrial town and railway junction of Oświęcim, known worldwide by its German name of Auschwitz. The camp consists of two parts, Auschwitz One and Birkenau. Both sites give a nightmare picture of one of history's darkest chapters.

A visit begins with a gruesome 15-minute film made by the Russians when they liberated the camp. Auschwitz was originally a Polish army camp, with brick-built barracks. The Nazis chose the site as a concentration and labour camp for Polish political prisoners, priests and intellectuals who were regarded as potential sources of resistance. Many of these captives were driven out to work in local factories. Hence the slogan over the entrance *Arbeit macht frei* - Work makes you free. It deluded prisoners into thinking that good work would earn their ultimate release. Later, Birkenau was constructed two miles away, as a camp for exterminating Jews.

8.5 Other excursions

Eight miles outside Kraków are the Salt Mines of Wieliczka, where a tourist route explores galleries and chambers on three mining levels. Visitors walk down 384 steps; otherwise it's walking on the flat. The return is by lift.

At this UNESCO Natural Heritage Site, extraction of rock salt began around 1290, and continued until quite recent years on nine levels that total around 120 miles of tunnels. There are underground chapels created by the miners, and an amazing cathedral with rock-salt carvings.

For a whole-day trip, a beautiful 67-mile road leads to the Tatra mountain resort of Zakopane. Here is traditional countryside with traditional wooden houses in an alpine setting. Zakopane is a thriving centre for walking, climbing and winter sports.